Take Two and Hit to Right

*Golden Days on the
Semi-Pro Diamond*

Hobe Hays

with illustrations

by the author

University of Nebraska Press
Lincoln and London

⊗

Library of Congress
Cataloging-in-
Publication Data
Hays, Hobe.
Take two and
hit to right:
golden days on the
semi-pro diamond /
Hobe Hays.
p.   cm.
"A Bison original."
ISBN 0-8032-7320-7
(pa.: alk. paper)
1. Hays, Hobe.   2. Baseball
players—United States—Biography.
3. Baseball—Nebraska—History.
I. Title.
GV865.H39A3   1999
796.357′092—dc21
[b]   98-45469
CIP

This book is dedicated to my father, Hobart Glen Hays, who loved baseball but, as a farm boy with adult responsibilities and a young family man during the Great Depression, had little opportunity to play the game. He made certain, however, that his two sons always did have that opportunity, and I thank him for this.

Contents

Acknowledgments   ix

Take Me into the Ball Game   1

Smokey Molden and Turning Semi-Pro   15

The Tony Sharpe Era   23

The Hired Guns Audition   33

Beginning Our Life in the NIL   41

Designated Drivers and Sinking Spells   55

The Left-Handed Legend of Lexington and Other Moundsmen   67

Box Scores, Base Hits, and Special Assignments   73

Baseball or a College Education—or Both?   85

Nebraska's Other Semi-Pro Leagues   95

Who Are Those Guys Anyway?   101

The Grand Island Incident   107

Nobody Had Seen That Kind of Power Around Here   117

You Can't Always Judge a Baseball Bum by Its Cover   127

Windy City Blues   147

The North Platte Years   157

Sand Hills, Sunshine, and Hard Slides   169

Roaring to Bankruptcy   183

The Party's Over   193

Stirring Some Hot-Stove Coals   201

The Big East and the Return to NILville   211

Appendix:

Nebraska Semi-Pro Leagues Team Standings

and Starting Lineups, 1948   227

Acknowledgments

I would like to thank the following people for assisting me in the preparation of this book: First, my wife, Bonna, who was so helpful and supportive in all ways. Two people from McCook, where my NIL days began, were the first to send me helpful information. Brent L. Cobb, news editor for the *McCook Daily Gazette*, and Marilyn Hawkins, of the McCook High Plains Historical Society, sent team pictures and *Daily Gazette* league information from the 1982 centennial edition.

Mr. and Mrs. Bill Denker helped me recall Lexington details and provided me with a rare photo of the legendary pitcher Lefty Haines. Another great NIL pitcher, Dave Garland, spoke with me about the "golden days" and told of a few key events that had escaped me. My brother, the semi-retired Rev. Don L. Hays, sent me a vivid memory letter about our NIL days.

Special thanks go to Andrea I. Faling, associate director of library archives at the Nebraska State Historical Society, for helping with Nebraska baseball history, and to Cynthia E. Monroe, Karrie L. Dvorak, Chad A. Wall, and the late Katherine Wyatt of the Nebraska State Historical Society reference room, where I spent so many hours in microfilm research.

Bob Grogan

Take Me into the
Ball Game

When Bob Grogan called me one Saturday in the spring of 1948 and asked if I wanted to take the Burlington train out of Lincoln with him for a trip to the wheat and cattle lands of McCook, Nebraska, I didn't realize I was to be part of a well-organized plan to "get" peerless Elmer "Lefty" Haines of Lexington and crafty old Walt Ibsen of Holdrege. Nor did I realize that the success of the plan was to Mc-Cook-area citizens second in importance only to getting the crops in. Or maybe it was the other way around.

"A couple of McCook businessmen came down to the university field after practice and asked me if I would play shortstop for them this summer," Grogan told me. "They said they would make it worth my time. Then they asked if I knew of a good second baseman."

"Where's McCook?" I asked.

"About 230 miles southwest of here," Grogan said.

I had played two years of semi-pro ball with Bob in Lincoln for Sandy Silverio's hardball nine, sponsored by Goetz Beer, and was in my second spring with him at the University of Nebraska. Bob was the best shortstop I ever saw outside of pro ball. We worked well together around second base and had always been good friends, so I didn't have to think very long before agreeing to travel to McCook with him for the tryout.

That decision let me in on the memorable summer when the Mc-Cook Cats upped the ante in the NIL, the Nebraska Independent League of semi-pro baseball. This league was to become so good within a year that hot-stove comparisons were made between it and the Lincoln Athletics in the Class A Western League of professional baseball, where future major leaguers Bobby Shantz and Dick Stuart and Hall of Famer Nellie Fox were beginning to get attention.

At the time of Grogan's call, I was twenty-two years old, and the exciting world of adult baseball was just beginning to open up to me. I thought back a few years, remembering a short—just over five-foot—fourteen-year-old kid entering Lincoln High from Whittier Junior High, crazy about all sports but physically destined to focus on baseball. I couldn't run for any sustained time without getting pains in my side and becoming very winded (exit basketball). I loved football and could pass well, even though the ball was too big for my hand, but wasn't heavy or big enough (I was a year too young for my class). I wasn't fast enough for track. And going to the same junior high with the kids from north Lincoln ("Roosian Bottom"), I had very little contact with golf. In fact, I seriously discovered golf only after my baseball playing days were over.

The Rock Island Railroad ran on a northwest course through Lincoln in those days, just missing Municipal "Muny" Park. I was never sure if I lived on "the wrong side of the tracks" or not. I was only a block away from my elementary school, Elliott, and only three blocks from my future high school, Lincoln High. We seemed to be about on the "cusp" in school districting, just slightly on the Whittier Junior High side. Getting there turned out to be the only long walk I had to school—ten blocks, and they were ten very cold blocks into the teeth of January and February subzero gales out of the north.

Although there were many sports that I liked but could not physically do well, I could always catch a fly ball. My dad taught me how as a preschool youngster, tossing me high flies with a tennis ball back in Bayard, Nebraska. Though I was born in Bethany, now part of Lincoln, we moved around where the jobs could be found; during my kindergarten and first- and second-grade years we lived far out in western Nebraska in tiny Bayard, where my dad found temporary employment in the post office.

My dad was very important in my sports development, more so

even than most dads. Having missed out himself as a boy—he had adult family responsibilities thrust upon him early on the farm—he was determined that my brother and I would not miss out too. He made personal sacrifices to assure us of playing time and opportunities. He once asked to be put on the night shift at his post office job so that he could help coach and transport us in the old '33 Nash to our loosely organized early baseball games.

My father was always there even though he never had enough sleep. I remember he would try to get some rest through those hot (without air-conditioning) summer mornings after coming home from his shift at the post office as the sun came up, and then get up only a few hours later to help us out with a game.

When I played at Nebraska U., he would take vacation time to walk over and watch the home games. I would see him sitting by himself out on the hillside slope behind right field. There was plenty of room in the bleachers, but he liked it out there. It made him feel more like he was in one of the games he had missed as a boy—a safety right fielder, possibly. Years later, when I too became a watching father, I liked to do the same thing—sit or stand down by the fence near an outfielder where I could hear the chatter from the players, far away from the annoying voices in the bleachers. It took me into the ball game again.

Dad wanted me to pitch. In his few chances to play as a young man, he developed a low sidearm knuckle ball, despite losing the third finger of his pitching hand to blood poisoning in 1932, when I was in second grade. He drove one-handed the 440 miles from Bayard to Lincoln in a 1928 Dodge, probably averaging less than thirty miles an hour, to have the badly infected finger amputated at the veterans' hospital before the blood poisoning spread and became a life-threatening condition.

I remember the four of us kids, ranging in age from three to eight years, leaning forward (we were afraid if we sat back, the car would roll backward downhill) in the back seat with our fingers crossed to help that old Dodge climb some of those Sand Hills grades, and my mother having to shift gears because it was Dad's right-hand finger that was swollen beyond saving. We had to make that tedious and nerve-racking journey to the Lincoln veterans' hospital because it was the only way we could afford the emergency medical care needed. Many times those narrow old wood-spoked Dodge wheels almost didn't make it through the deep western road ruts.

While my dad recuperated from the operation on his right hand, we took up temporary residence in the basement of Grandma Thomas's house in Lincoln. It was in the middle of the Great Depression, and times were very tough. Above us in the one-story house lived several of my aunts and uncles while they all worked and helped one another through the University of Nebraska. Aunt Dorothy Thomas wrote numerous short stories that appeared in top 1930s magazines—*Colliers, Saturday Evening Post, Harper's, Ladies' Home Journal, Woman's Home Companion*—and several books, including *The Home Place* and *Ma Jeeter's Girls*, published by the University of Nebraska Press. As a result, her financial help was critically important to her brothers' and sisters' pursuit of college education. They never forgot it and repaid her later when they became successful professionals.

Once Dad was able, he worked on road construction crews and as a timekeeper at the rock quarry near Roca, Nebraska, while he and Mother tried to map out the best future for our basement-dwelling family of six. They decided not to return to Bayard but to stay in Lincoln and find an inexpensive house. They located one at 24th and L Streets, and our life in our own home began in 1934. After several temporary low-paying jobs, my dad landed a full-time position at the Lincoln Post Office, and we celebrated as if we had won the lottery. Even at the age of eight I could sense the enormous importance of this blessing of job security.

It was shortly after this memorable day that my baseball career resumed. Harrowing economic problems temporarily solved, I could afford the luxury of thinking of sports again. It was then that I noticed the wonderful location of the house my parents had selected, at least from my standpoint. Directly across 24th Street, then a gravel road, Antelope Park ran parallel to the creek north and south, giving us three-quarters of a block of wonderful, tree-shaded space to play. And across a small metal bridge was "Muny"

Park—a collection of four softball diamonds and one baseball diamond—which presented Lincoln twilight men's baseball, American Legion baseball, and Lincoln night league fast-pitch softball. All of this, I soon discovered, was almost more than I could consume, even with my enormous appetite for the national pastime.

Summer was a wonderful time for me again. I could go just across the road and play catch with my brother or, when we could get a third player, grab a bat and have batting practice with a backstop on a vacant diamond at Muny. It was a great way to learn how to place hits, with only one fielder. When we collected another outfielder, we could swing away. In just a year or two, I began to qualify for the more organized aspects of the junior baseball teams that were being formed.

As for my own pitching, I had one brief summer in the sun, in one game at Muny Park striking out fourteen of my thirteen-year-old opponents with a surprisingly big-breaking curve. My fast ball didn't worry anybody, but most of those boys just hadn't seen a curve ball and were bailing out. I soon discovered, however, that pitching wasn't quite right for me because I wanted to be on the field every game and I liked to hit.

I had learned to bunt well from the teaching drills of old Ike Evans, Lincoln's Pied Piper of youth baseball in the 1930s. Ike was a man in his sixties who seemed to be on a one-man mission to teach young boys how to play. He had written and published a thin handbook and had become a self-made program, promoting baseball, coaching, and transporting sandlot boys to games, giving them something of a schedule before the Junior American Legion, Midget, and other baseball programs came into existence and became popular. At the end of the summer we looked forward to the Ike Evans special treat: an enormous, thick milkshake at Brick's ice cream shop.

Since I was small, Ike always told me to crouch down and work out a walk. I hated this, because I wanted to swing, but I did learn the strike zone by looking at a lot of pitches. Bunting, to Ike, was the most important part of the game, and he conducted countless bunting drills with all the boys. I never regretted it because later on I became a very dependable player when the need came to lay one down.

Ike never actually bunted a ball for us. His hands shook so badly with palsy we all doubted if he could bunt one fair, and we never pressed him to try. But he would show us over and over how to crouch and square around on the pitch, how to hold our arms out away from our body, and how to cradle the relaxed, horizontal bat loosely between the thumbs and first fingers. We got the idea, and we could all bunt.

I started in right field—not that anyone thought I had a strong arm; the theory was that fewer balls were hit there because everybody wanted to pull the ball for power, and most of the kids hit right-handed. They all thought because I was small I couldn't catch a ball. Little did they know how advanced I was at judging fly balls. But after a few games in right field I felt a remoteness, a lack of involvement in the game, and I began plotting my way into the infield, where I thought the action was. I didn't have the arm for third or short, but since the ball came off the bat the same way at second as in right field, I adapted well to this position. It didn't take me long to become as good at picking up ground balls as I was at getting under fly balls.

As a boy who grew up in a small one-story house with my parents, one brother, and (by 1937) four sisters, I knew what it was like to be part of a very close family. I think the convenience of the baseball and park facilities was a blessing for all of us. It certainly was for my mother, since it provided a constant outlet for my brother's and my bursting energies and frustrations and in good weather kept us out of the house doing what we loved to do (winters were a little more of a problem).

Adjacent to the center-field fence of the main diamond was Muny swimming pool, which I visited infrequently because of my concentration on baseball. In fact, I didn't learn how to swim until I was eighteen and in boot camp, where, following U.S. Navy nonswimmers policy, they pushed me into the ten-foot end of the pool to force me to swim. I nearly drowned in that terrifying event, unable to come to the surface despite a desperate flailing of arms and legs. Finally, a bamboo pole was poked down to my floundering body. I seized the pole and climbed it to the surface just as my lungs seemed ready to explode. Exhausted and furious, I sat on the concrete pool side and glared at the navy bully in charge of nonswimmers.

"Now do you believe me?!" I gasped, chlorine water spraying from my nose and mouth. "I can't swim! I can't swim!" The wide-eyed, shocked faces of those naked (they didn't provide us with bathing suits in boot camp) witnesses of the near-disaster seemed thoroughly convinced, even though the bully, trained in the "sink or swim" school, still seemed confused.

It was the one-on-one teaching of Jim McAndless, state back-stroke champion from Stockton, California, that finally got me out of boot camp by showing me how to use water as a buoyant, support-ing friend rather than a terrifying element to flail and slowly sink through. I passed the navy's test of treading water for ten minutes, without using a swimming stroke, thanks to Jim, who first taught me how to "skull": sitting in the shallow end of the pool and staying off the bottom by simply moving one's cupped hands back and forth. After I learned how to do this astonishing trick and went on to float-ing on my back and treading water, I was able to leave boot camp in Farragut, Idaho, with all my friends, instead of being left back with strangers until I had learned how to swim.

I never forgot Jim McAndless, a quiet guy I really didn't know very well but one who took the time to help me beat my fear of wa-ter. Many of my friends from boot camp wound up with me on the uss *Wiley*, DD 597, headed for destroyer duty in the Pacific, but I never saw Jim McAndless again.

If I wasn't playing baseball myself at Muny Park, I hung about the fences at night, spitting sunflower seed shells on my shoes and watching the outstanding fast-pitch softball league. On the nights when the Ford team's Al Spaedt hooked up with fast Freddy Fuller and threw heat from down under, the Muny field was completely ringed by excited fans.

I not only loved sports; I also loved to draw and studied news-paper artists closely. One of my favorites was a political cartoonist from the *Des Moines Register* named J. N. Darling, who signed his name "Ding," a newspaper contraction. His work was published in the *Lincoln Journal*, a Republican paper, and my dad, being a Democrat, bought the *Lincoln Star*. I, in my compulsion to see Ding's latest cartoon, would sneak up on our Republican neighbor's porch, carefully unfold the paper, and study the front-page drawing, my heart pounding. Then I would refold it just as the paper boy had and leave it in exactly the same spot.

At the age of sixteen I drew several sports cartoons, one of the NCAA track meet held in Lincoln and another of our American Legion baseball team. I took the track meet drawing to sports editor Walt Dobbins at the *Journal*. He looked at me dubiously, then back at the drawing: "You did this?"

I nodded yes. After some further assurance Walt called a photographer in, my picture was taken, and my first big-time newspaper cartoon was published the following Sunday with my picture and a short item that incorrectly said I had been interested in sports "only the last couple of years." Four years later, when I returned from the war, I became "Star Sports Staff Artist" while I went to the University of Nebraska, drawing NU sports figures for *Star* sports editor Norris Anderson. This time I held out for money: $10 per drawing.

In 1942 Los Angeles played St. Louis in Hastings, Nebraska, in the western regional playoffs of the American Legion baseball tournament. Brother Don and I, over the objections of my parents, hitchhiked the hundred miles from Lincoln to see the game. It was the last time I ever hitchhiked on the highway, because we narrowly escaped death or serious injury when the careless driver who had picked us up decided, to our terror, to pass a car at the crest of the hill on the two-way road (which they nearly all were at that time). At that exact point another car sped to the top of the hill from the other direction and, in order to avoid a head-on collision, whipped his car off the road and into the ditch, then luckily back onto the highway. No one spoke during the rest of the trip to Hastings, and we never told our parents about this incident.

Standing next to the backstop during batting practice, after some of the color had returned to our faces, Don and I marveled at the power of hitters from both teams. Talk floated about, and I listened in on everything I could. One major topic of conversation was the left fielder for St. Louis, who was called a natural, pure hitter. Another was the catcher for St. Louis, who was sure to be signed before the end of the tournament. What actually happened was that the pure-hitting outfielder became a great catcher, and the sure-to-be-signed catcher wound up a journeyman receiver who moved into broadcasting and was known as Joe Garagiola. The natural-hitting outfielder, later converted to catcher, was of course Yogi Berra.

A year later, when I was seventeen and had finished my senior year at Lincoln High (where I suddenly grew to the height of five-foot-ten), I played my last year of American Legion ball with the Lincoln Blues. We were a pretty good team that summer of 1943, and in the state tournament at Norfolk we advanced through the first round to play Neligh. I was still doing some pitching then and started the game against this "sentimental favorite," as the *Omaha World Herald* labeled Neligh. I can only suppose it was a "sentimental favorite" because of its size, but Neligh did have something going for it that the big-town Lincoln team didn't: a ballplayer named Richie Ashburn.

Ashburn was from Tilden, but through some legal shuffling he was allowed to play for Neligh. In the seven-inning game I pitched well enough to last through five, allowing only one run and five hits. Jack "Nick" Brady and I exchanged places in the sixth; I went to left field, and he took us home with his good fast ball, allowing no hits and no runs the last two innings. Since our team was leading 2 to 1 when we switched, I was the winning pitcher, with a final score of 3 to 1. Ashburn got two hits off me—both singles—and I collected two myself off Neligh pitching. I think that might have been about the last time I pitched, since my desire from then on was to play second base. It was a nice way to end my pitching career—beating a team with a future Hall of Famer on it.

Later that month, after we beat Hastings and met the Omaha Vikings, who beat us for the American Legion state championship, Omaha organized its first state American Legion All-Star benefit game. I was chosen as an alternate to represent our Lincoln Blues team. Warming up before the game, I heard talk of a catcher who had a number of major league scouts looking him over. The word was he had a great arm, could hit, and was very fast. When infield practice started, I realized they were talking about Richie Ashburn.

Since Richie was so fast, I had wondered ever since we'd beaten Neligh in the state tournament why they had him catching. I suppose at that level of ball, having a player who could throw runners out with a strong, accurate arm and who was smart and could stay cool under pressure to help the pitching was really the top priority. But apparently the same thought I'd had about Richie's speed passed through the Phillies management's thinking when they signed him, because from then on Richie played center field and did so with the speed and skill that put him into the Hall of Fame in 1996.

Among my memories is a learning experience that occurred during my brief action in this game, one that I remembered all through my playing days every time I was near second base with a glove on. It was a slow ground ball to short with two outs and a runner on first. I raced over to cover as the shortstop fed me an underhanded toss. I paused, caught the toss, put my foot on second, and lingered a moment to be sure the umpire saw it clearly. The next thing I knew, I was catapulted fifteen or twenty feet into left-center field. I landed on my right shoulder, still clutching the ball tightly, and quickly got to my feet. The wide-eyed shortstop and second-base umpire asked me if I was okay as I walked back to the infield, and I said I was. My biggest surprise was that though feeling a bit strange and unable to let go of the ball when the umpire asked for it, I did not hurt anywhere. Later I found out that the runner who had lowered his shoulder into me was an all-state fullback from Omaha South, manufacturer of some of the toughest football players in the entire country—including Tom Novak, all-American great center/linebacker/fullback who would later star at Nebraska. From then on there was no second baseman in the game who got away from the base quicker than I after making a play.

After the American Legion state tournament that year I was invited to attend the Chicago White Sox tryout camp. I think the scout was impressed with my fire and energy that day. I had yelled myself hoarse trying to encourage our big left-hander, Morris Galter, who had a world of stuff, to find the plate. Poor Morrie walked nine, hit Bill Danze twice, and wild-pitched six times in that game, which we lost 10 to 1. To show what kind of stuff Galter had, even though he only pitched one out into the fifth before being removed, with all that wildness he still struck out six. I felt so bad and helpless for old Ralph "Pat" Thacker, our coach, as the smart Omaha Vikings just kept taking strikes before they would even swing, and the runs kept walking home. Jim Sharp, who later would play with us at Nebraska, mowed us down with his good fast ball enough times to keep us from ever getting in the game.

I felt proud about the scout's invitation but didn't go to the camp, since I had planned to go directly on to college. It had never been my intention to try for a career in pro ball. Later I reminded friends of my wise choice. "All I would have had to do was beat out Nellie Fox," I noted.

If I had a favorite major league team then, it was the St. Louis Cardinals, simply because at that time they were the closest team to Lincoln. And I liked the cardinal on their uniforms, Diz Dean, Enos Slaughter, "Ducky" Medwick, Pepper Martin, and their "Gas House Gang" image of wrong-side-of-the-tracks, underdog guys. I identified with them more than with the powerful, always well-stocked and machinelike New York Yankees, who were also much too far away to care about.

Ralph "Pat" Thacker was the most important influence during my American Legion playing years, and one of the most memorable in my life. Somehow he became coach of our team at an age when most folks of his years would consider rocking on the front porch a stress test. My first memory of him is of a stocky, slightly bowlegged old guy in a cream-colored wool baseball uniform and cap, slowly making his way across the Lincoln High baseball diamond (where we practiced and played) in the 90-degree afternoon heat of midsummer. He introduced himself to the team and then mopped his face and head with a huge white handkerchief.

"Sweating is good for you," he said. "It's when you don't sweat that you have to worry."

Pat Thacker did not have to worry. He was sweating plenty, and it was no wonder: I learned he had walked ten or twelve blocks from his home in south Lincoln in full uniform. I can't remember if he had his spikes on or not.

As the days went by I began to listen more carefully to what this very soft-spoken (I almost had to learn lipreading) ex–Triple A, American Association third baseman said. Each practice added to my belief that I was hearing baseball wisdom I would never get from another source. I leaned in closely when he told funny stories from his playing days with some of the "coo-coos," as he always called them.

"Al Schacht was a very funny baseball clown," Pat said one day, "but Nick Altrock was the best. And he was a very good juggler, too." I had always heard that Schacht was the king of baseball clowns. I had never heard of Altrock at that time, but since then I have read much to support Thacker's opinion.

Then, switching from storyteller to coach, he would talk about how the game should be played. "How much does a baseball weigh?" he would begin. "Several ounces? You can easily lift it with two fingers, right? So why do you need to take a running start after you catch a fly ball to throw a runner out? Why does a pitcher pitch from the stretch position with runners on? So they can't get a good start on him to steal. When these coo-coos today catch a fly and then take two steps and a hop and a skip before they throw the ball, the runner is nearly halfway to the next base.

"A pitcher from the stretch position can throw almost as hard as with a full windup. He does not lose a whole lot on his fast ball. You're not throwing a javelin or shot put. When the ball is hit, run hard to get under it, stop and get into throwing position with your weight on your back foot, like a pitcher in the stretch position. Catch the ball and then, like a pitcher, step and fire off the back foot to the cutoff man or base. Whatever speed you lose on the throw you will easily make up for with the quicker release, and the ball will get there sooner."

To this day, at any level of play, I rarely see outfielders heed this very sensible, scientific advice. Most of them, even in the majors, waste critical moments from the time the ball hits their glove by hopping and skipping before releasing a throw. I thought Pat was right then, and I still believe he was, even if hardly anyone seems to coach or do it his way.

Pat Thacker also had his own theory of how best to get back to first on a pick-off throw from the pitcher. "You take your lead and get set, with your hands hanging down, not on your knees," he would say. "At the first move to throw over to first, you do the cross-over step, dig the right foot in, and hook-slide into first. Simple—step, slide, and you only give the first baseman your toe to tag."

We spent hours talking. He did most of the talking; I watched his mouth and listened closely as he wove a rich fabric of life with the Triple A "coo-coos" and shared coaching gems found in no book on baseball.

"Did you ever watch a sprinter in a track meet?" he would question. "What are his arms doing when he's going full speed? They're relaxed and swinging in counterbalance to his stride. Why? Because that's the way he can get down the track the fastest. Do you ever see one racing down the track with one arm stretched out high in front of himself? Not often, because all the other sprinters would pass him.

"How many times have I seen an outfielder run for a long fly ball with his glove hand reaching way out in front of him, as if by waving his glove at the ball he can make it fall down into it. Usually that fellow doesn't get to the ball before it drops, because holding his arm out front has reduced his running speed too much. When you are eating dinner, do you open your mouth when you stick your fork into the food on your plate? Not usually. Most of us put the fork into the food, bring the food up to the mouth, and then with perfect timing open the mouth and put it in. We don't behave like baby birds with their bills stretched open, cheeping and hoping the mother bird will poke some food into it. The way to catch a fly ball is to run like a sprinter to the ball, then reach up and receive the ball like taking food off your fork, in a natural, efficient way, not like a baby bird."

At that time I was playing some outfield as well as second base and still trying to pitch. From that day on, whenever I chased a fly ball I made sure I was not a baby bird, floundering across the outfield with his open stretched bill cheeping for a worm.

Pat Thacker was a Renaissance man among old baseball players; he understood the physics, psychology, biology, sociology, and fine art of baseball. Walking about slowly in his spikes, he shared what he knew with those wise enough to stop and listen.

In fact, throughout that summer I sensed I was getting rare information very few people would ever hear. I would listen as long as he talked, even after the other players had gone home, and then watch Pat go off across the Lincoln High diamond with his slightly bowlegged gait. In his Minneapolis American Association wool baseball uniform, he probably caused people who saw him moving along the south Lincoln sidewalk to think he was the biggest "coo-coo" of them all. But I never did. Without that uniform on he just wouldn't have been Pat Thacker, the man who helped me climb under the fence to the magic of early big-time baseball.

Smokey Molden and
Turning Semi-Pro

The first time I was paid to play baseball, and thus became a semi-pro, was in June 1946. I was twenty years old and had just been discharged after two years in the navy, including nine months' duty on the uss *Wiley*, DD 597, a destroyer in the Pacific fleet. The war was over, and while waiting to take the "cattle train" from San Diego to the St. Louis Separation Center, where I would be discharged, I had played some second base with the San Diego Naval Base team—not a lot, because they had Ray Feracco and a few other infielders who had played pro ball.

Back home, I was watching my brother Don, who was a little too young to have been drafted for World War II, taking batting practice with Sandy Silverio's semi-pro team on the main diamond at Muny Park in Lincoln, Nebraska.

"Take two and hit to right," Sandy yelled to my little brother. Don took two good rips and drove a couple through the left side of the infield. "Run this one out, Donnie," the stocky Cuban ex–second baseman shouted. Don punched the ball into right field and dug for first. "Get the piano off your back!" Sandy instructed in a voice heard clear across town. "You run too long in one place!" Then he looked at me. He knew about my having played a few months with the San Diego Naval Base team. "Get in there and hit, Hobie. Let's see what you've got."

I stepped in from the right side and glanced at the mound, where a tall, lean right-hander studied me with a smile. I had noticed earlier that he was black, which in Lincoln in 1946 was very uncom-

Smokey Molden

mon on a baseball diamond. I picked up the first pitch, a three-quarter sidearm delivery thrown with a big, easy whip action. It seemed to be right over the middle, and I turned on it with confidence and made contact. The ball felt like it had been left out in the field all winter in a cold rain. My hands vibrated—if it had been a cold day, they would have been numb—as my first effort bounced indifferently toward short. After a dozen less than impressive attempts, I finally drove one with authority out of the infield. I slipped away from the plate while I was hot.

"What's he throwing?" I muttered to my brother, rubbing my hand full of "bees." "I can't get any wood on the ball!"

My brother grinned. "The ball sneaks in on your hands, doesn't it?"

"Yeah," I said, "and it's heavy! Who is that guy?"

"That's 'Smokey' Molden," Don replied. "Wait until he throws hard."

It was the next Sunday that I saw him throw hard.

"We're going to *Eu*-reaka," Sandy announced.

"Where?" I asked my brother.

"Utica. The game's in Utica."

That Sunday afternoon in *Eu*-reaka Molden threw smoke, and I watched in fascination from my second-base position. We all watched. There was very little action except on the mound and behind the plate. I had no idea at the time, but there at the beginning of my eight-year semi-pro career I was playing behind very possibly the best pitcher in the state, pro or semi-pro.

We drove to other towns around Lincoln and Omaha that summer, playing for gate receipts—60 percent to the winner and 40 to the loser. Brother Don and I would pick up anywhere from $7 to $20 a game in the smaller towns, more on the notable contests with traveling teams at Sherman Field and Muny in Lincoln.

I continued to study Molden with admiration bordering on awe throughout the summer of 1946. Smokey was a friendly person to be around. He didn't have the intimidating stare of most hard throwers. It was more like seeing Ernie Banks out there on the mound. I thought about how easily Smokey smiled and decided that if I knew I could throw the ball by three out of four batters everywhere I pitched, it would be very hard to wipe the smile off my face.

That next spring I started as a freshman at second base for the University of Nebraska. Bob Grogan was starting shortstop, and Don would letter as a utility player. Don and I would drive down to Muny Park following university practice in 1947 to work out with Sandy's team, which was getting ready for the semi-pro summer. After hitting line drives on the NU diamond, I would go down to Muny and hit bouncing bricks off Molden.

"These damn bats don't have any wood in them!" I exploded one evening after hitting Molden's offerings every place on the bat but the right place. Bill Kinnamon, Sandy's burly veteran catcher (later to umpire in the American League), roared and nearly fell out of his shin guards laughing.

"No wood!" he echoed. "These bats have no wood in them!"

I turned away, completely red-faced, realizing the busher absurdity of my college hotdog remark, and never again mentioned equipment failure in connection with my inability to hit Smokey solidly.

Kinnamon was one of the finest high school catching prospects in the Midwest until he broke both his legs in a bad car accident. He could still hit and had a great arm, but never regained his foot speed.

It was soon evident that Smokey could blow away guys from *Eu*-reaka and David City and York and even Omaha with regularity, but I wondered just how good he really was. And I wondered why he wound up in Lincoln playing for a peppery Cuban with a beer franchise and trouble pronouncing Nebraska town names. It was only then that I took note of something that I, like many others, had somehow overlooked: major league baseball was all white. After considering Molden's options then, just before Jackie Robinson broke the color line, I understood. Smokey picked up very good side money—semi-pro pitchers took home large portions of the 60–40 gate—driving to nearby towns on Sundays and after work and pitching. Negro league traveling teams, on the other hand, drove grueling hours on old buses, often playing more than one game in more than one town on the same day, sometimes for little pay, and without access to public food and rest stops. It was impossible for those players—unlike Smokey—to hold another job at the same time.

Sandy proved to be a very sound Lincoln businessman as well as a solid supporter of live local baseball. The enterprising Cuban realized that right after the war he could put together a very capable ball club on short notice and take on all comers, and with Smokey on the mound he had an excellent chance of winning. He got in touch with all the top traveling teams in the country, starting with the House of David and the Oakland Larks. Booking games to coincide with the traveling schedule of the Class A Lincoln Athletics allowed Silverio to play at the Lincoln A's ball park, Sherman Field, where he could draw some impressive gates.

The Oakland Larks, West Coast semi-pro champs, came into Lincoln with a thirty-three-game winning streak in 1947. Sandy sent Smokey out to break that streak, and he did—in thirteen innings with twelve strikeouts, giving up just one run. Next, Molden scattered seven hits and coasted to an easy 12-to-2 win as Sandy's Goetz team jumped on the House of David pitching for thirteen hits. After that, Smokey led Sandy's nine past Roosevelt Post of Omaha, 8 to 2.

But the real tester, the one to measure Smokey's true ability against the best, came in the form of the Kansas City Monarchs. The celebrated Negro league Monarchs had a regular team and a traveling team, both made up of outstanding players. That night they had their own "Smokey" on the mound, named Steve Wylie. The supporting lineup included Willard Brown, great center fielder, who had a batting average of .355 after playing eleven years with the Monarchs and two with the army; he went up to the major leagues later in 1947. Alongside him was Hank Thompson, who, records show, hit several long home runs off Bob Feller in off-season black-versus-white, head-to-head pitching contests between Feller and the fabulous Satchel Paige. Catcher Earl Taborn was good enough to be given a contract with Newark in the Triple A. Othello ("Chico" or "Chappy") Renfroe was the hard-hitting second baseman, Roberts played shortstop, Souell third base, Cooper first base, and Scott left field. (A year later, "Cool Papa" Bell, said to be the fastest base runner ever, even faster than Ty Cobb, and mentioned in the same respectful tones as Paige and Josh Gibson, would be managing that traveling Monarch team.)

As Smokey warmed up that night at Sherman Field, you couldn't help noticing some of the Monarchs paying close attention to the tall, black right-hander whose loose, whipping fast ball exploded like a big firecracker when it hit Kinnamon's mitt. Bill knew just how to make the ball pop the loudest, and you could see a contented smile on his face when it happened (nobody wore a mask then to warm up a pitcher—even when it was Smokey Molden). By the time the game started, a lot of interest from the Monarchs' bench was focused on Molden. Except for a few turns in life, Smokey might very well have been warming up on the Monarchs' side of the diamond.

As we took the field, a roar went up. I glanced at the stands, and my eyes opened a little wider when I saw how packed they were. Not even the A's drew like this. There was a secret pride in Sandy's dusty uniformed locals, and Lincoln fans had turned out to see just what Smokey could do against the best traveling team in the country—maybe the best in the world.

I tried to settle myself down. I had never looked out from behind the pitcher and seen so many people. I glanced out to left field where Dick "Dr. Strangeglove" Stuart of the Class A Western League Lincoln Chiefs would hit most of his record sixty-six home runs for one year (1956), and then back to the mound where "Wee Bobby" Shantz of the Lincoln A's would set them down with big stuff before going on up to the Philadelphia Athletics.

Smokey finished his warmups, and Kinnamon's cannon throw to second stung my hand. Tense with excitement, I flipped the ball to Grogan. Relax, I said to myself. You're only playing a team with a few guys who would probably be in the majors if they weren't black. I smoothed out a spot with my spikes where Nellie Fox, destined to the Hall of Fame, would soon patrol with more skill and success than I.

Smokey held the Monarchs scoreless until the fifth inning and had a two-hitter until the sixth, but then their vaunted power and

Wylie's three-hit pitching won out over the game's local favorite. Nevertheless, Smokey proved that night that he could, for a time, hold his own with the nationally celebrated Kansas City Monarch team.

After Grogan, Don, and I signed with McCook the next summer, I lost track of Smokey, though I know he continued to pitch in and around Lincoln for a while. But I never forgot the night at Sherman Field when he threw smoke past the Monarchs for five innings and drew such a great crowd that the Hays boys took home their biggest single-game share of their baseball lives to date: $52 each.

Bill Denker

The Tony Sharpe Era

Late in February 1947, following my first summer of semi-pro baseball, a meeting was held on the second floor of the old basketball Coliseum at the University of Nebraska to introduce a new baseball coach, young William D. "Tony" Sharpe, twenty-eight-year-old former Cincinnati minor league infielder.

As I looked around the room that cold night, I felt a quality of excitement and purpose, and I also noted a great deal of life experience in the large turnout. Nearly all the players were World War II veterans going to college now on the GI Bill, the government program that paid for the tuition and supplies of veterans who qualified. Nebraska, a cold-weather state, had never carried the reputation of a baseball powerhouse—the last conference championship had been in 1929—but something gave me a strong feeling of optimism. Even my optimism, however, didn't begin to match the actual accomplishment over the next four years of this collection of talented and experienced athletes, hungry after the war's interruption to play civilian baseball again, as they had done as boys.

The season began with a lot of unknowns, but soon a few facts were established. This team was going to be a contender. It would be a new team and a strong team; few of the previous year's lettermen would even make it. The infield had an unusually hard-hitting shortstop, Bob Grogan; a slugging third baseman with a strong arm, Bill Denker; a very tall defensive ace, Bob Schlieger, at first; and me, a capable pivot man who could get on base and score runs, at second. The outfield was led by future major league slugger Bob

Cerv, high-average line-drive hitter Fritz Hegwood, and strong-armed funny guy Jim Sharp, who kept us all loose. Big Jim Sandstedt and Elroy "Lefty" Gloystein gave us excellent veteran pitching; and football quarterback Sam Vacanti and Del Blatchford, steady catching. Lefty was twenty-seven years old, and Jim was just a few years younger.

On the field, Tony Sharpe immediately established an atmosphere of the high professionalism he had absorbed from two years of playing infield in the Cincinnati Reds minor league system. Tony showed us how to suit up—how not to "break" the cap bill but bend it carefully into a curve, how to fold the length of our pants to mid-calf so we wouldn't look like bushers, and how to fix our socks so they wouldn't fall down even if we had to run out a triple. We all respected this quickly, impressed as we were with having a former minor leaguer to coach us. We had come to play ball, and we could see we had somebody to lead us who knew what he was doing. We got down to business right from the first practice and became more confident by the day as Tony took us through professional drills and even pitched us good curve balls himself in batting practice.

He showed us how to hit behind the runner and was one of the best himself, timing in a little shuffle step that would delay his right-handed swing so that he could drive the ball into the hole between first and second. Tony was hoping that I would catch on, but I, seeing Cerv, Denker, and Grogan—our middle-of-the-lineup sluggers—pull the ball with such power and get admiration and attention, wanted some of the same. Hitting to the opposite field always looked to me when I was a kid like the hitter couldn't "get around" on the fast ball. Regretfully, it took me some time to appreciate the value of moving the runner up by Tony's technique.

When we got behind in a game, Tony would be up on his feet shouting out to us, "Come on out there! Don't get your daubers down! Make some noise, Hobe! Let's hear something!"

"Daubers down?!" The only "dauber" I had ever heard of was a "mud-dauber," a black, nervous wasp that always had something up high on his tail end. I decided Tony's expression meant, don't quit working. Keep daubing the mud, and don't get tired and discouraged.

Bill Denker, over at third, would call out to us in the infield, "Bow your neck! Be tough, now!"

And from the outfield, smiling Jim Sharp would shout, "Ahoya! Go for two. Let's be double players!"

Keeping my dauber up and my neck bowed was a little tiring, but it did make me tougher on defense. At least I thought so.

Then Bob Grogan at short, in a voice barely audible, would say something that sounded like "Wheedle-deedle, wheedle-deedle," and I would think, what? Later I figured out that he was saying, "Wheel and deal it, wheel and deal it" to the pitcher.

Tony would shout again to me, "Make some noise, Hobe. Let's hear something!" and I would say, "Have a life!" (shrill whistle, without fingers in my mouth) and "Shake it up!" But apparently my voice was too deep to carry very far, or else I didn't know how to project, because Tony would be right on me again a couple of batters later. On the bench between innings I would tell Tony that I *was* talking it up, in fact yelling myself hoarse, and he'd say he couldn't hear me. Frustrated, I began a study of how to make my voice carry better.

One time when it was Lefty Gloystein's day to start on the mound for us, he sat on the training table before the game with trainer Buck Barger working on his neck. Tony, who could look worried after a 10–0 shutout win, walked over to Lefty.

"How do you feel, Lefthander?" he asked, trying to smile. Lefty reached up to his neck carefully.

"I've got this crick right here. I can only turn my head this far," he said. "My shoulder tightened up last night and is a little sore."

"How's your lower back?" Tony said.

"Sore," Lefty said. "But we're working on it."

"And the pitching finger?"

"About the same. I'm going to soak it." Tony patted the trainer on the shoulder.

"Do what you can, Buck," Tony said. "I'll check back later."

I looked at Tony, who I thought would be fumbling for the antacid pills, but to my surprise I saw a tiny smile at the corners of his mouth, even though the rest of his face still wore the "what else can go wrong?" look. I walked out of the training room behind him.

"What do you think, is Lefty going to be able to start today?" I asked.

"Oh yeah," Tony said, laughing. "Lefty will probably throw a three-hitter this afternoon." I was confused. "If," Tony went on, "Lefty ever tells me he feels great, I'll know we're in big trouble."

Lefthander did go out and pitch a fine game, nibbling at the corners with that good curve ball and keeping the hitters off balance with his heady pitching. I don't remember seeing him wince or hold his neck or shoulder once. And he bent his lower back just fine on his follow through.

We didn't tear up the conference that first year, but we played like a professionally coached team with great potential, which is what we were.

The next spring the addition of power-hitting catcher Tom Novak, a great team leader and future football all-American standout, was enough to move our performance up a notch. We would get a couple runners on, and Tony would yell to us on the bench, "Come on now! Ducks on the pond! Somebody knock them in."

In one of those situations, Tom Novak picked up a bat and headed toward the plate. Bill Denker shouted, "Come on, 'Tug', you're due! If you don't bring them around, I'll kick you in the uterus!" Tom smashed one into the gap in right center, and two runs scored.

Some fans were surprised that burly Tom Novak, who would hit .351 in 1949 for the Huskers, could play baseball so well, but Tom was a product of the Omaha American Legion baseball system, which was one of the best-organized -coached programs in the whole country. Teams like the Omaha McDevitts and Vikings and players like major league flame-throwing right-hander Rex Barney (Bob Feller once said nobody threw any harder) come to mind immediately.

Tom was a great leader and by example pulled everyone along to do just a little better, hurt or not. After watching "Trainwreck" in action on the football field, taped from head to foot and hobbling, you just didn't complain of a sore arm or a sprained ankle. Tom was the toughest dude of all.

Tom and Bill Denker, who was also a little rough, enjoyed each other's company and would often sit together in the bus and carry on periodic conversations through the long, sleepy miles of those college baseball trips.

"Shakespeare!" Tom would announce suddenly.

"What is it, Aristotle?" Denker would answer.

"I would require thy attention. Get thee hence and pretend thee to listen," Novak would command.

"Shut thy ass, my Lord," Bill would respond. "I am perchance trying to sleep." The bus would rumble on while Aristotle pondered his reply, finally deciding sleep was after all a better choice for himself, too.

Nebraska center fielder Bob Cerv was an exceptional athlete. From Weston, Nebraska, he brought the skills of baseball and basketball to the Cornhuskers and was a standout in both those sports. He was such an explosive home run hitter that big league scouts were soon camping by the fence making rapid notes.

But I, and I imagine many others, often wondered how Cerv would have done at halfback or fullback on the football team. With his speed, quick starting ability (he was an excellent base stealer), and the running power of 196 pounds of compact muscle, he would have been a backfield coach's delight. In the late 1940s there were not many fast backs in the country carrying nearly two hundred pounds; this was a good weight for a lineman in those days. In the early post–World War II years the Big Red football program had yet to enjoy the Bob Devaney years of greatness (1962–73).

Starting out on one road trip to Boulder to play the Colorado Buffaloes, we noticed a snowflake or two passing the bus windows. It was early in May, so nobody had taken seriously the forecast of possible snow or even a blizzard. But about five miles west of Seward, Nebraska, the snow increased and soon was whipping by our now darkening windows. Before long we were driving in near-zero visibility, and the highway was completely hidden under several inches of wind-whipped snow. Larson, our trusty bus driver, wisely pulled off on what he hoped was the shoulder, flipped on the hazard lights, and waited while we rapidly discussed our options.

As the snow increased to a startling blizzardlike intensity, Coach Sharpe soon decided that we should turn around and get back to Lincoln while we could. We all strained our eyes to see if the highway was clear enough of traffic to turn around, and Larson began shifting gears and trying to point the big bus back eastward, but it became stuck. First we all went to the back of the bus over the drive wheels to put as much weight on them as possible, but that didn't work. It was then decided—I believe by Shakespeare and Aristotle—that all of us would get out of the bus fast and push it around before somebody came out of the zero visibility and crashed into us. We all scrambled for any position where we could touch the bus.

On the decided count we all heaved, and Larson gave it the gas. Wheels spun. Snow flew—wet snow with stinging force—and the bus moved a few feet. Some of us lost our footing and flopped on our faces but quickly got to our feet to help keep the big bus moving. We went down again. We got up again, pelted from the waist down with a spinning blast of gravel and new snow, and when we slipped lower, we were stung in the face. We finally inched the bus around onto the highway and scrambled back on board with Tony Sharpe shouting for us to hurry up. We began cautiously rolling our way home, Larson and all of the team and Tony straining for signs of the edge of the highway.

I was always grateful that we had Shakespeare and Aristotle to bring out enough adrenaline and dedication to get the huge bus moved around and headed for a dryer, safer place. Actually, if necessary, I believe Novak, Denker, and Cerv could have done it by themselves.

The early spring of 1948 was highlighted with a ten-day trip throughout Texas, Oklahoma, and Kansas. A two-game series with Southern Methodist proved to be one of the most interesting stops because our opposition included an all-American named Doak Walker, who excelled in football and was definitely going to the National Football League but was also playing center field for the SMU baseball team. Most of us had heard of Walker's fine athletic achievements and potential, but not until talking to him after the game were we aware of his charisma. Cheerful and friendly and with square-jawed, rugged good looks, Doak and his very attractive girlfriend lingered to talk with us about his NFL plans and other topics. The all-American could still wear the same size hat, and the fact did not go unnoticed.

Later, Bob Grogan said to me, "Walker is sure a nice, happy, friendly guy, isn't he?"

"Yeah," I said, not recognizing my dour envy, "what's he got to be cranky and unhappy about? He's only got a beautiful girlfriend; he's the all-American big man on campus starring in two sports; he has an NFL contract waiting for him; he's good-looking, well built, and has some family money—I believe I could force a smile myself with all of that." Grogan thought this was funny. He didn't usually talk a lot, but on the bus I heard him quoting my observation to other players and enjoying another laugh with them.

I remembered thinking as I watched Doak getting a lead off first before he tried to steal second (I can't remember if we got him or not), how is this average-sized guy with just pretty good speed going to make it in the NFL? Or even what did he have that made him all-American? Maybe if I had had to tackle him instead of just tag him, I would have answered my question quickly. Having watched both Walker and Bob Cerv take a lead and come down to second on a steal, however, I believed I would rather try tackling Walker than Cerv. Walker might have made me miss, but Cerv would have dislocated a few parts of my body.

It would seem that I inherited much of my mother's temperament. She came from a family of ten children—seven brothers and two sisters—and had spent some years as a young child growing up in the wilds of Canada. Her father died when she was ten, and with the help of the older boys her mother took care of all ten children after they moved back to Kansas.

My mother, who had six children of her own, always hated anger and conflict. To a certain degree, I followed her pattern of tolerating people's differences, avoiding conflict, and playing the game of baseball with the artist's eye for the action and design of the game. Vince Lombardi's "Winning isn't everything, it's the only thing" came very slowly to me if at all, for I enjoyed the aesthetic aspects of the game: a beautifully executed double play, a great one-hop throw right on the base to cut down a runner, a smooth hook-slide around a tag, an echoing double down the left-field line. If these also produced a win, so much the better. If they didn't, a three-for-four at the plate, all hit on the nose, and an errorless day in the field that included a couple of sparkling double plays were enough to send me home happy. I had to work at needing to win to be satisfied. Tony Sharpe once exclaimed to me in great dismay, "If I could just get you mad every game, you could be a hell of a ball player!" And I was thinking, hold that pose, Tony, while I sketch that expression (I was the only art major on the team).

Strangely enough, winning was almost always there when I played baseball; maybe that's why I didn't have to focus more attention on it. At NU we won two conference championships in four years. At McCook we won one NIL championship and two Shaughnessy playoffs (moneymaking postseason elimination games among the top four league teams) in three years, and at North Platte it was two NIL championships and one Shaughnessy playoff in three years. With Sandy Silverio's Goetz team behind Smokey Molden, it had been almost all wins. I suppose the fact that I was a starting regular for all these teams is some testimony to my team value. Even so, I was made aware that I was not sufficiently "full of piss and vinegar," so at Nebraska I set out to develop a meaner face at game time. My first Harpo Marx idea of a fierce expression was quickly dismissed, but I gradually developed an attitude more dedicated to victory first and foremost, and damn the aesthetics.

In a game against the Oklahoma Sooners in Norman, a mysterious thing happened which remained a mystery for years. I had sprained my ankle in the previous game and wasn't sure I could play. Buck Barger, our trainer, taped it thoroughly, adding extra strips for good measure. I tried the foot out carefully during infield practice, noticing that it bothered me some if I tried to go to my right and stop suddenly, but I started the game.

The first time up I hit a hard ground ball directly at the shortstop, who had a very strong arm. The pitch must have been on the outside of the plate, because I was leaning toward first when I hit it and came out of the box like a shot. I relaxed and lifted my knees smoothly so as not to hurt my ankle and found myself flying down the line as if blown by a very strong tail wind, which that day was nowhere to be found. The shortstop fielded the ball cleanly and made his usual strong throw. I was out by less than half a step—I had almost beaten the throw! I went on down the line, carefully gearing down so as not to roll the ankle again, and then jogged back to our bench, wondering if anybody had noticed what just happened.

"Sprained ankle, my ass," someone said. "You never ran that fast in your life."

"Yeah," another said. "You should sprain your ankle every game."

I was bewildered but secretly delighted. I had run for thirty yards like Harry Meginnis and Dick Hutton, sprint stars on the Nebraska track team, though I had never been accused of resembling them out of the blocks before. For the first time in my life, running had seemed right, my stride smooth and even instead of slightly off as if I needed a tune-up. I'd felt I was hardly touching the ground. I honestly had never known that feeling before.

"What's all this bull about a sprained ankle?" asked another voice from the end of the bench.

"I don't know," I said, still baffled but holding back a smile. "I didn't feel a thing running straight forward, but when I try to cut, or stop suddenly, I feel it might go."

I sat down and continued to ponder that miracle trip down the first-base line. I had no answers. I had definitely run faster than ever before in my life, and I felt a sense of urgency to discover the reason before the whole experience vanished, never to be found again.

After the game I sat in the dressing room staring at the magic tape on my ankle. It had to be the tape; it was the only factor that was different. I was afraid to cut it off for fear I might lose that speed forever.

In later games I began taping my ankles, partly to protect them from my tendency to sprain them but secretly to try to catch the magic speed again. The ankles felt secure and firm, but my speed remained about the same as usual. I concluded sadly that I had lost the magic forever.

It was years later that I solved the mystery of "speed for a day," and by that time it was too late; my playing days were over. It took an X-ray of my spine to put me on the trail. A chiropractor I consulted about my chronic early morning backaches discovered that I had a lateral curvature of the spine because my right leg was three-eighths of an inch shorter than my left leg. He prescribed a heel lift inside my right shoe to make up the difference and raise the right side of my pelvis slightly in order to straighten my curvature gradually. This did relieve my regular morning backaches and, curiously, the bloodshot eyes I was always troubled with when standing on my feet.

Later on I tried brief sprints with the lift in my sneakers, and I could feel that smooth stride again of the ninety-foot "magic" sprint. Taping both ankles had not changed anything because it only maintained the original difference between my heels. Taping only the right ankle that day in Oklahoma had created the effect of the lift, especially with the extra tape that Barger had wrapped under my right heel. Imagine my revised scouting report if I'd only known this sooner: "Average arm, contact hitter with warning-track power but Meginnis-Hutton speed!"

In 1948 Nebraska won the Big Seven Conference championship and then played Oklahoma State in the interconference regional play-offs at Sherman Field in Lincoln; we lost in an exciting third game. Then we all prepared for a summer with our respective semi-pro teams in the Nebraska Independent League, the Pioneer Nite League, and the Cornhusker League. Coach Tony Sharpe himself took a few grounders during practice and prepared to play shortstop and third base for David City in the Pioneer Nite League. It was a great year for young Coach Sharpe: it had been nineteen years since Nebraska had won the conference baseball championship.

The Hired Guns Audition

As Bob Grogan and I stepped from the hissing train into the sleepy McCook dawn that early May morning in 1948, I heard a rooster crow behind the station. It had been an all-night ride from Lincoln for two tired infielders who had journeyed 230 miles for a Sunday morning tryout on the McCook Cats, cellar dwellers of the semi-pro Nebraska Independent League.

The McCook Baseball Board was already convinced that Grogan was their man at short but wanted to see what I looked like at second. They couldn't wait until our season at the university was over, so they bought us a round-trip train ticket to come out on an open date for a workout.

We still had a few very important series in the Big Seven, which was becoming a very exciting race, and there were semester finals, so we could not move to McCook yet even if approved. We could not even play with the McCook team until our college season was over (though some got around that rule by playing under fictitious names for a few games).

The McCook Cats were going for broke that summer and wanted to nail down their starting lineup as soon as possible. They had heard some very good things about Grogan and didn't want anyone else stealing him from under their noses, so the plan was for us to come for a tryout, eat dinner, and sign a contract, then take the Burlington train back to Lincoln and finish up the college schedule.

After stretching our legs from that all-night train ride and getting our bearings, as the glow of dawn welcomed us to the Red Wil-

Bob Grogan and Hobe Hays

low County town of McCook, Grogan and I walked two blocks up Main Street to the Keystone Hotel, where a room had been reserved for us. We checked in and went upstairs to try to get a little sleep before the late morning tryout. We must have felt like two hired guns coming in to straighten out the town.

We were starting to settle down for our nap when I noticed what looked like a hole in the wall. Out of curiosity I went to examine it and found that it certainly was a hole in the wall, about the size of my little finger. My curiosity getting the best of me, I peeped through it and to my astonishment saw a man and a woman lying side by side on the bed "naked as jaybirds," as I would later hear it described in McCook. At that moment, as if on cue, the woman decided it was time to fool around again and signaled her desires to the man, who obediently rolled over to provide his services.

"What's in there?" Grogan said.

"Nothing," I whispered.

"Then why are you whispering?" Grogan whispered. "Let me look. Come on, what do you see?" After a few more seconds I backed away carefully, and Grogan took his turn at the wall. He looked up at me in amazement and then back to the peephole. After a few seconds I tapped him on the shoulder.

"Come on," I said. "It's my turn."

"Just a minute," Grogan said, refusing to budge.

"Hey, come on, Bob, I discovered them. Besides, you're married. This is old stuff to you."

"Yeah, but I like to know how others do it." Finally Bob backed away and gave me the "your turn" sign—but both people were gone. I heard the shower running.

"Nice going," I said to Grogan. "Thanks a lot."

We really didn't have much time to sleep before the workout by then, but we tried. I kept thinking about what had just happened. What were the odds of getting a hotel room with a hole in the wall looking right in on the bed in the next room? Probably the only room in the hotel with a hole in the wall. And what were the odds of a couple lying naked in that bed in that very room, performing for us, when plenty of other rooms were empty in the hotel of this very small town?

Was this a secret but standard procedure of the McCook Baseball Board to provide entertainment for prized recruits and paint a promising picture of interesting adventures in the future? Who were these two people? Hired performers for special occasions such as this, or simply a mysterious couple from out of town, meeting for a secret rendezvous?

Was this just pure coincidence? A completely accidental, chance, one-time happening, having nothing to do with an entertainment committee or planning? And if the hole in the wall was so obvious to us, why hadn't this couple seen it too and covered it if they were seeking privacy? And why hadn't they heard us scuffling for position at the peephole, even though we were trying to keep our voices down?

Whatever the explanation, it was the most unusual morning either of us had experienced in some time, one that would make the hitting and fielding of a baseball later that day no small challenge in concentration. Neither Bob nor I spoke to each other about our theories concerning this bizarre experience. I think we each preferred the scenarios of our individual imaginations.

At the time of our arrival, the morale in McCook was very low because its team had finished last in the NIL the previous two years. Since the board had heard that Bob "Spider" Grogan was another Marty Marion, the St. Louis Cardinals' rangy shortstop (a fair scouting report, except that I thought Grogan hit the ball harder), I knew I had to resemble at least faintly the Cards' sure-handed second baseman, Red Schoendienst, if I wanted to stay.

Apparently I had something that caught their eye, because they not only signed me up but asked if there were any more like me at home. I said, yes, my younger brother Don, who would be starting third baseman at the University of Nebraska if it weren't for having to beat out the best man at third in the Big Seven Conference, Bill Denker, who had already been signed for the summer by the Lexington Minutemen—another NIL team. Brother Don went out a few days later, took batting and infield practice, and was hired to play third base in the new McCook adventure. I forgot to ask Don if he had a hotel room with a hole in the wall, too.

Since before the Depression and on into the postwar 1940s, town baseball had been the number-one sporting interest—and to many, gambling interest—of all small midwestern communities. Rivalries were intense and long established, and if you were standing in just the right places, you could see large sums of money passing hands behind the bleachers in years not stricken with grasshopper plagues and droughts.

The years after World War II became the Golden Age of Nebraska semi-pro baseball. Many players returned with valuable baseball experience on strong service teams, and all came home with a hunger to play baseball again in a peacetime setting.

The three best semi-pro leagues in Nebraska right after the war were generally agreed to be the Nebraska Independent League, the Pioneer Nite League, and the Cornhusker League. The NIL would become the most freewheeling, notorious, expensive, and in the opinion of many the best of the three. The very factors that gave it this distinction would also hurry its inevitable destruction.

The NIL was first assembled in 1935 with eight teams representing Holdrege, Lexington, Kearney, Grand Island, Boelus, Oxford, Eustis, and Sumner. For the following twenty years the league fielded several combinations of teams, but Holdrege, Lexington, and Kearney held fast throughout the prewar and postwar years as solid members, except for Lexington's absence (for financial reasons) in 1951.

In 1936 North Platte became a member, and Sumner and Grand Island dropped out. Two years later the league tried out Broken Bow, Ogalalla, and Gothenburg to work with the solid three. McCook became a member in 1940.

The NIL performed in the late 1930s and through 1941 with other state leagues such as the Big Six, the Big Three, and the Kansas-Nebraska League. Then, like most of the country, in 1942 the NIL went to war and didn't reassemble until 1946, when the towns of

McCook, Holdrege, Lexington, Kearney, Hastings, and North Platte formed a six-team postwar league.

The 1946 season opened with the North Platte Flynns against the Hastings Aces and their star pitcher, Harry "Hippity" Hopp of Nebraska football fame. The following year North Platte became the Plainsmen and kept this name until the end. Hastings, now the Sultans, after winning the 1947 NIL title, dropped out of the league because of a money shortage. In 1948 the NIL comprised the Mc-Cook Cats, the North Platte Plainsmen, the Lexington Minutemen, the Holdrege Bears, the Kearney Irishmen, and a newcomer, the Superior Knights.

In 1949 the addition of Grand Island and the return of Hastings for another try made it an eight-team, two-division league. The following year it went back to the six teams when Grand Island and Hastings failed to survive financially.

The year 1951 was a turbulent one: the NIL played without the usually present Lexington and lost Superior in midseason over a serious difference in league structure and playoff specifics. An extremely wet early season rained out so many games that makeups were nearly impossible to complete, and gate receipts—always necessary to float the teams—were washed away.

The following year Lexington rejoined the NIL, the weather was much better, and the six-team league was healthy and back in business again for a few more rip-roaring years—until its eventual self-destruction.

The 1948 season was a turning point. The McCook situation had become intolerable to the town merchants and nearby farmers who had suffered regular losses in betting transactions and were having to pass up the tempting odds offered by gloating high rollers from out of town. The crisis desperately called for imagination and sacrifice, so "Doc" Dennis, the best dentist in town, sat down with "Pat" Patrick in Pat's shoe store to plot some emergency action and formed the McCook Baseball Board. The plan was simply to raise enough money to hire "the kind of team that couldn't lose very often," so that Doc, Pat, Big Bill Hanke, and the old boys in new blue overalls, who came in from their big cattle ranches or rich cropland to hang around P. O. Karthauser's pool hall, would all get well at last.

The Baseball Board had little trouble selling the plan to go out and buy the sort of team that couldn't lose very often. The merchants of McCook and a few wealthy farmers and ranchers agreed that immediate and speculative action was needed, so they contributed what they could to build a payroll. This way they thought it might be within the realm of possibility to get back at the dreaded Lefty Haines of Lexington and Walt Ibsen, the ageless right-hander from Holdrege, who both still had too much stuff for any home-grown baseball team. The table was now set for revenge in McCook. It was payback time for hungry baseball McCooksters, and they anxiously awaited their new mercenaries' return in a few weeks for the NIL summer.

Al McElreath

Beginning Our Life
in the NIL

Although the 1948 regional playoffs between the Cornhuskers and
Oklahoma State were exciting and important, and we were disappointed—after taking a first-game lead—to lose the series in a
close final game, I must admit that between games I was looking
ahead to my first summer in the highly respected Nebraska Independent League. It was going to be exciting and rewarding to receive a regular monthly check, win or lose. I honestly don't think it
affected our postseason college play—and I say "our" because most,
if not all, players in our starting lineup at NU were headed for a
semi-pro summer similar to mine. The boys from our opposition in
all probability looked forward to a similar summer in Oklahoma as
soon as their postseason play was concluded. Once our college season had ended, we could all concentrate on our semi-pro jobs.

I had heard that the NIL pitching was good, even better than
that in the Class A Western League. Would I be able to hit this
pitching? We had faced some pretty good pitchers in the college season, but the word was, out there in the NIL it came from outstanding veterans of both semi-pro and pro experience and a few college
aces.

A few days after our 1948 interconference college series ended,
brother Don and I arrived in McCook, suitcases in hand, to take up
residence for our first NIL summer. We were told to look up a Mrs.
Pearl Fagan over on West Fourth Street, who would rent us a nice
basement apartment and give us the option, which we accepted, of

eating a boardinghouse-style supper with several other folks. Mrs. Fagan also ironed shirts for a very reasonable fee.

After resolving the housing situation, Don and I looked into daytime employment possibilities, because almost all our games would be at night. Since in 1943, before being drafted, I had worked with Cy Sherman, legendary sportswriter for the *Lincoln Star*, I thought I would see if there were any part-time openings for reporters at the *McCook Gazette*.

I was able to set up an interview appointment with the mysterious and aged editor-publisher, the intimidating Harry Strunk. After an hour in which I convinced Mr. Strunk that I was a serious student of journalism, an all-round American lad who would never, ever become a baseball bum, tall Harry, his long, leathery face smiling and frowning at the same time, thrust out a weathered hand and congratulated me as a new member of the *Gazette* staff at $25 a week. When word of my salary leaked out, I was reasonably certain, there would be no bitterness or jealousy from the other staff members.

But I was delighted to get the chance to write for the sports page and learn more about newspaper work. My duties were to cover all McCook NIL games and compile statistics, write a few non-sports features when called on, and produce a sports column twice a week. And since Les Spence, the sports editor, already had a column on general local sports, it was decided that I would focus on special-interest stories about the NIL to generate interest and make the fans more optimistic about their refurbished team's future. It suited me just fine to do a little public relations work and have fun writing too. (Brother Don started off with a Nehi pop bottle-washing job but soon got a sore arm and switched to work better suited to saving his arm: delivering furniture!)

At the typewriter that first morning trying to compose my column, "Sports Haze by Hobe Hays" (named by Les Spence), my mind drifted off to 1943 in the *Lincoln Star* office of the gruff, hard-working dean of Midwest sportswriters, Cy Sherman, who sat at his massive Underwood typewriter and puffed on his cigar as he wrote his column. One day a middle-aged man in a brown suit and hat appeared in the doorway. Cy got up and talked to him in the hallway for a while, and then the man left. Back at his typewriter, Cy looked over at me and grunted through his cigar, "Do you know who that was?"

I thought hard a moment. "No," I answered.

"That was George Sisler," Cy snapped, and began typing again.

I stared at the doorway where this average man in the brown suit had stood and tried to remember everything I had seen, since to me—at age seventeen and living in Lincoln, Nebraska, far from big league baseball—this graceful fielding and great-hitting Hall of Fame first baseman was indeed a legend and the first major league player I had ever seen in person. I felt that moment as if I had seen a ghost—but a ghost of surprisingly average and mortal proportions.

Cy Sherman was a man to whom all Nebraskans owe a great debt of gratitude. He was the writer who changed the name of the University of Nebraska football team from the "Bug Eaters" to the "Cornhuskers."

Until 1948 most of the NIL teams were made up of local ballplayers, but soon the character of the league changed radically. Two new and predominant elements were added: ex-professional ballplayers from every class up to the majors, and veteran outstanding college players recruited from far outside the local territory.

The older ex-professional ballplayers who drifted from town to town, playing baseball for money and working at odd jobs, became known as "baseball bums" by established senior citizens (a very small group) who cared less about the improvement in local baseball than retaining the quiet and predictable character of their towns. The "college hotdogs" (so named by the baseball bums), who rented rooms and also worked at summer jobs, were treated with just a shade less suspicion than the baseball bums by these town-integrity residents.

Those two groups made up the nucleus of the Nebraska Independent League from 1948 through 1955, producing such a profound change in the quality and cost of NIL baseball that the "semi" in "semi-pro" became a joke to sportswriter Barc Wade of the *Kearney Hub*, who wrote in July 27, 1949, "They used to call this the Nebraska Independent Semi-Pro League, but now it hardly falls short of the professional status. Several teams have payrolls that would make a Class D league team's look like a dollar to a dime."

The NIL towns were located about midway between Lincoln and Denver, whose teams in the Class A Western League offered the closest possibilities for southwestern Nebraska people to see good professional baseball in those pre-television 1940s. Since either city represented a trip of more than two hundred miles for most, the NIL emerged as a near-satisfying substitute.

In those days McCook was a town that saw a lot of rocking and resting going on among the older folks on hot summer afternoons. Most of the younger people had gone to other places for summer job or college opportunities. There were few exciting or controversial events—except for the Chamber of Commerce "donkey baseball" games; the infrequent visits of big bands such as Blue Barron, Horace Heidt, and Jan Garber; and "Golden Spike Days," which featured mandatory growth of facial hair for men on pain of a dunk in a horse tank on Main Street. To twist a well-known sentiment, McCook was a nice town to live in but you wouldn't want to visit there.

So the town inhabitants needed a focal point such as a ball team to rally around. On the day of a home game, stand-up signs at downtown intersections read "Baseball Tonight," and to nearly everyone this was "the only game in town." Special incentives for the players to excel were painted on the outfield fences in some parks. The McCook businessmen offered, "Hit me and win a new pair of shoes" or "a deluxe dinner for two" or "a case of Nehi pop" (soda to easterners) to hitters who banged the walls on the fly at the designated areas. There was something very warm and special about those town fences with their individual personalities. A home run was not just hit over the 350- or 375-foot marker; it was hit over the Patrick Shoe Store sign or the Nehi sign.

In early June the setting of the summer sun assured at least a slight drop in temperature throughout McCook. On that night of the first home game in 1948 an excited hush cloaked this small NIL town. Those signs at main downtown intersections announced an event that would bring an overflowing crowd to little Eastside Ballpark: "Baseball Tonight." Nothing more was needed; everyone in town knew what baseball, and with whom. They all knew it was the night for Lexington and Lefty Haines, or Holdrege and Walt Ibsen or Art Dollaghan, to drive into their town and try to wrest a victory from their battling Cats.

Deep into July and August the setting sun no longer assured any measurable temperature change. Heavy warm air would hang over the town throughout the night. There was no air-conditioning and no television in the modest southwestern Nebraska homes that year. McCook people sat on porch swings or porch steps, waiting to catch the smallest breeze. Inside the houses, electric fans tried to circulate and cool the air enough to let folks get to sleep when it was time. Radios would be turned up and windows raised so those on the porch could listen to Jack Benny or Bob Hope and the Pepsodent show. Later in the evening dance music from Chicago could be captured with careful, crackling tuning. Russ Morgan's or Blue Barron's big band faded in and out across the Midwest air waves. From a small record player over on West Fourth Street, Kenny Sargent sang "Under a Blanket of Blue" with Glen Gray's Casaloma orchestra as Pearl Fagan and her daughter Beryl, their work finished for the day, sat on the porch and fanned themselves with folded newspapers.

In fact, the Eastside Ballpark remained one of the coolest places in town. But on this mid-June evening in 1948, the heat was not on anyone's mind. The game was the thing. Excitement of this degree had not been felt around Eastside in a long time. After finishing in last place in 1946 and 1947, the McCook fans had been promised a completely different outcome in 1948, with three new infielders from the Big Seven college champ, the University of Nebraska; an outstanding former Triple-A pro outfielder; and an ace pitcher secured from the 1947 NIL champs, the Hastings Sultans.

Don and I walked from our car to the McCook dugout on the third-base side of the infield. I picked up a ball and lobbed it to Don, and we began to loosen up our arms.

Tall, thin, and stooped Carl "Whitey" Skoog, pioneer McCook ballplayer who had been selected to manage the Cats that year, came over to me with a stocky thirty-six-year-old, medium-sized outfielder who was ready to take his batting practice cuts. His name was Al McElreath, and he was from Muskogee, Oklahoma. Al was new to McCook, just as we three from Lincoln were. He had played pro ball in the Southern League with Chattanooga and Memphis, leading the league one year in hitting. He had also played for Sacramento, California, in the Triple-A Pacific Coast League in 1944–45 before coming to the NIL. He had a carefree smile, strong forearms, and a very strong grip.

We talked a little, and then he began singing softly to no one in particular, "I will be your rooster, if you'll be my hen. I'll come 'round and see you, every now and then—" After that he stepped to the plate and began smashing left-handed line drives off the outfield fence. The sound of that ball echoing off his bat around the wooden outfield fence was a memorable experience. When he finished, I walked by him, my ears still ringing. He smiled, winked, and said, "That's the way we hit them in Triple-A." Then he continued singing softly as he walked away, "Ain't gonna' be no other chickens hanging 'round but me," and I stepped in to show how they hit them in the college hotdog league.

Al kept a huge first baseman's mitt out in left field by the fence, and while everyone focused on the pitcher getting the sign from the catcher, he would put it on and nonchalantly hide it behind his hip, where his finger glove was rolled up and stuck in his pocket. When a fly ball came his way, Al's much longer glove helped him make up for the step he had lost in all those years of pro ball. After catching a fly ball and firing it back to the infield, he quickly switched gloves again before someone could spot an irregularity. And playing outfield with a big first baseman's mitt fell into that category in those days, even though today all gloves are that big or bigger.

P. O. Karthauser—I never learned just what the P. O. stood for—was next up for batting practice. I had met him before when I tried out for the team, and I didn't want to shake hands with him again; I was still trying to get my knuckles back in alignment from the last time. Karthauser was about an even six feet tall and very, very solid. When he walked out to the plate in his protective catching gear, he walked "heavy"—heavier than his 190 pounds. Some athletes walked tough; P. O. walked heavy. The earth didn't exactly shake, but you felt, after watching him advance to his defensive position, sliding his mask over those narrowing eyes, that he was not going to be the one to move in a collision at home. His throw to second was much like Bill Kinnamon's of Sandy Silverio's team: it got there in a hurry, and it stung the glove hand unless you let your arm hang loose like a chain.

P. O. was a permanent resident of McCook and a few years earlier had been good enough to figure strongly in the Brooklyn Dodgers' catching plans—until he disappointed them by settling down to operate a pool hall and lunch counter in this small town. He had acquired the nickname "Bowser" because when he shouted through his mask to get some life out of the infielders, he sounded like a huge dog with a husky throat.

Karthauser had a very hot temper, which he worked to his advantage with the umpires. He would often fake a tantrum with the plate umpire just to stir up the opposing fans; at Holdrege they became so caught up with emotion that they held scheduled "Boo P. O. nights." Since the umpires were never quite certain when P. O. was just giving the fans their money's worth and when he actually was upset, they kept their masks on during these very realistic performances. Karthauser was as tough as his name sounded. He was a take-charge guy on the field, a man with a twinkle in his eye and a friendly smile in the pool hall.

Eddie Miller played center field for the McCook Cats—before, during, and after McCook began its very active outside recruitment. Throughout the years many players were replaced at McCook, but at no time did anyone think of trying to improve the position in center field. There just wasn't any need. About six feet tall, Eddie was fast and had an excellent throwing arm, accurate and strong; he was the perfect center fielder. He could make a one-hop throw to third from right center a thing of beauty, and at the plate his slight uppercut on his swing would propel the ball high in flight over the outfield wall. He was speed, power, energy, and athletic grace on the ball field. And he smiled a lot. It was more like a grin, as if he had just discovered how great life was. He did enjoy life, and baseball was a big part of his. Ed was also a very funny storyteller, sharing with us the tales he picked up from the town's master yarn spinners while working in the family grocery store in McCook.

When a home game was rained out just before game time, it was always a letdown. We didn't know what to do with ourselves, so some of us who were single would cruise Main Street—all the way north and back down to the south end by the railroad station. I'm not sure what we thought we were looking for. I think it was girls, but we already knew most of them were not in town; they were away at summer school, working at Estes Park in Colorado, or never here in the first place. I don't know where or how we thought they would suddenly appear; I think if we had ever actually found one or two strolling down the sidewalk, we would have run into a lamppost. I don't remember doing any serious looking, anyway, because I knew we would all wind up playing pool and having a beer at P. O. Karthauser's place.

The rich odor of fried onions and hamburger delicately wafted through the thick cigarette and cigar smoke at P. O. Karthauser's pool hall and grill at the south end of downtown McCook in mid-June of my rookie NIL year. The clacking of pool balls burst through the muffled chatter of the hall's regulars—older men in overalls and straw hats playing chess or dominoes at small tables—and, on off nights at the NIL ballparks, young men in short-sleeved sports shirts with the sleeves turned up two folds. A few of these young men were longtime inhabitants of the town; the rest were temporary town dwellers, hired for the summer to help win baseball games in the NIL.

One regular at P. O.'s leaned over the main pool table near the front door and banked the four ball cleanly into the side pocket. He walked around to the other side of the table, his jutting jaw clenched on a short cigar as he sized up the shape he had left himself with, and chalked up his cue for the next shot.

"Might as well rack 'em up," P. O. said. "Old Sarge is going to run the table." I looked over at the table where a wiry forty-eight-year-old with a white crew cut and wearing army tan clothes, looking older than he was, methodically began to destroy his opponent. I had been in town only a few days and hadn't yet spent much time in the pool hall, since I was neither a beer drinker nor much of a pool player.

"How do you know that?" I said. "Is he that good?"

"Yeah," P. O. said. "Sarge spends all his time in here. I think you could call him a hustler." I glanced around the hall to see who was there. The Cats' first baseman, Gene Dellenbach, hung up his cue from another table and walked over to us. Back at the main table Sarge hadn't given up his turn yet, and he was working on the last two balls.

"How you shooting tonight, Gene?" I asked.

"Not good," Gene said. "I'm not seeing them right tonight. Could I have a beer, P. O.?" Karthauser popped the lid of a Pabst Blue Ribbon and set it down with a glass in front of Gene.

"How's your ulcer, P. O.?" I asked.

"Oh, not so good, Hobie," P. O. said. "I've got to watch the fried foods."

"It couldn't be your hamburgers. Man, they're too good," I said.

"Well, they're not good to me. Something sure isn't."

I didn't think it was the fried foods as much as it was the stress. Even as he bounced around the pool hall with that heavy step of his and big smile, there was a deep crease in the center of his forehead. Business didn't seem to be going so great, and I'd heard he had other problems. He poured himself a glass of milk and leaned on the counter.

"Where's Donnie?" he said.

"I don't know," I said. "I thought he would be in here—he shoots a pretty good game. Maybe he's got a date."

"You know," Gene said, "the other night after the game at Eastside, Donnie came off the field and a girl from the bleachers met him. They walked to his car, and sitting inside was another girl waiting for him."

"That's why you can't find any girls, Hobe. They're all in Donnie's car," P. O. said.

"Yeah," I said.

"Do you want a beer, Hobie?" P. O. asked, taking a big drink of the rich milk.

"No thanks," I said. Eddie Miller walked through the door and came over to us, smiling as usual.

"What's this about Donnie having two girls waiting for him in the car after the game?" Eddie said.

"There was only one in the car," I said. "The other one was in the bleachers."

"You going to shoot some pool?" Eddie said, looking around to see if there were any empty tables. "P. O., give me a beer. Hobe, you want one?"

"No, I don't think so," I said. "I'm kind of restless tonight. I think I'll go out and walk around some and then maybe I'll come back and shoot a little pool." Dellenbach put his bottle down.

"I'll play you a game, Eddie," he said. "If you can't beat me tonight, you never will."

"O.K., Gene," Eddie said. "Hobe, have a beer first. "I'll buy you a beer."

"No, Eddie, I don't drink."

"One beer won't hurt you! Make that two beers, P. O." I really didn't drink. I had gone all the way through two years in the navy and never had a drink. It was just one of those things from home—we never had alcohol in the house, my mother being the daughter of a preacher and very strongly against alcohol and tobacco. P. O. set the two bottles of Schlitz and a Pabst on the counter. Eddie took several swallows from his bottle and turned to me with his happy grin. I studied my bottle a moment, took a sip and held it in my mouth, then swallowed. Eddie watched me and saw my face register the bitter taste.

"Not like that!" he said. "Drink it down, like you would water. Take a couple of big swallows! Don't hold it in your mouth first." I tried it Eddie's way, and it didn't taste so bad. I tried it again, and after about two-thirds of the bottle I really didn't think I needed to go out and take a walk. Eddie and I leaned on the counter and talked about the last game, and the hamburger and onions never smelled so good. P. O. brought us another two bottles of Schlitz, and the pool balls clacked above the soft humming of the ceiling fan and the chatter and occasional bursts of laughter from the men in overalls and straw hats.

"See that guy over there in the overalls, eating a hamburger and looking over those card players' shoulders?" Eddie said. "How much money do you think he's worth?"

"Well," I said, "he doesn't look like he has much. But since you ask this question, I would say probably more than I think."

"He's about the richest guy in the western part of this state," Eddie said. "He probably owns about a third of Nebraska."

P. O. came over to us pressing his hand against his stomach. "Goddamn ulcer," he said. "I knew I shouldn't have had that cheeseburger with onions." We talked some more about baseball and about the girls that weren't in town, and P. O. set two more beers in front of us.

"Wait a minute," I said.

"On the house, Hobie. You are no longer a college hotdog. Tonight, you're a beer-drinking baseball bum." Eddie turned, grinning, and looked over his shoulder.

"There's Donnie now," he said. "He's over there playing snooker." I was feeling strangely mellow and perfectly content to be standing at the counter on one leg with my foot going to sleep, and just hearing the ceiling fan and the clacking of the balls behind me. I no longer felt restless and had no intention of wandering out into the lonely town.

"Guess who he's playing," Eddie said.

"Who?"

"Sarge," Eddie said.

"Jeee-e-e-z," I said, without turning around.

I ordered a hamburger with onions. Soon brother Don joined us. It hadn't taken Sarge long to put him away.

"Hobe, you drinking beer?! Since when?" Don said. "P. O., give me one of the same." Eddie grinned.

"How'd you do, Donnie?" he asked.

"He beat me," Don said.

"How much did you play for?" I asked.

"Ten bucks," Don said.

"I should have told you Sarge is a pool hustler," Eddie said. "When he wants to play, there's nobody around here that can beat him. He lives in this pool hall."

We drank our beer and both Don and I thought about our special evening in P. O.'s pool hall.

"I shoot a pretty good stick," Don said. "I thought I had a chance." I had to admire my little brother's guts, even though I frowned at his blowing $10 to a pool hustler. I wouldn't have taken on Sarge— but then I was never much of a gambler. I was the big brother and still thought I was supposed to look out for both of us. It was hard, but I was slowly learning to let go of that responsibility, which had somehow been delegated to me as a young boy and had become a pain in the ass to my little brother. Don insisted I no longer had to look after him.

Eddie Miller was grinning at just being alive, and at that moment I think I understood Eddie's philosophy more than at any other time. The ceiling fan hummed, the pool balls clacked over the sizzling of the onions, and everything just then seemed to be just right. Any problem that needed to be worked out would have to wait until tomorrow. It was a good feeling, and one I wished I could have taken out of the pool hall into the next day.

Warming up on the McCook sideline at Eastside before our next home game was a quiet and businesslike right-hander with a very smooth delivery. His name was Bill Gardner, a tall, thirty-nine-year-old control pitcher from a small hamlet just east of McCook called Holbrook. Gardner lived an unassuming life running a small grocery store there, but when he closed up shop and took to the mound, baseball-minded farmers packed up their families and drove miles to watch him pitch. As I watched over Bill's left shoulder from my second base perspective that season, I was convinced there was no more perfect pitching machine performing in the Midwest. And in 1948 McCook had him.

During one game against North Platte early in that season, Bill was looking so outstanding that I thought, what the hell is he doing out in that little town of Holbrook, or even here playing for McCook? Why isn't he doing this great stuff for some pro team that could really use this kind of pitching? I knew he was thirty-nine, but he was in great physical shape and still had it all. His fast ball was on the inside corner, then on the outside corner—never over the fat part of the plate. His curve ball broke sharply off the plate right over the low outside corner or froze the batter into taking it on the inside corner.

In about the eighth inning of that game we all realized he was pitching a no-hitter. Then in the ninth, suddenly there were two outs and we all got up on our toes for that last out to give him the special prize. Gardner threw just the pitch he wanted and induced an average ground ball straight to me. I must not have charged it quickly enough, because I took it on the in-between hop, and it bounded to my left off the heel of my glove. I pounced on the ball quickly and flipped to Dellenbach at first, but the runner beat the throw. "I blew it!" I thought. "Now the next guy will hit a dunker over the infield, and the no-hitter is gone!"

I was never more impressed with Gardner's poise and control than on the first pitch to the next hitter. He delivered his good fast ball right on the low, outside part of the plate, and the ball came off the bat right to me again. Bill wanted me to have a chance to make up for the boot. This time I came through, and I ran over to Gardner to congratulate him.

"I'm sorry, Bill," I said, "I almost blew your no-hitter for you. Nice pitching!"

With the calmest and sincerest look, Gardner turned, a little surprised, and said, "Oh, that didn't mean anything to me. Forget it." I was absolutely certain he meant it. A no-hitter at Eastside Ballpark against North Platte in 1948, before the wild "arms race" was at full speed, really *didn't* mean anything to him. If it had been Double- or Triple-A ball, I'm sure he would have been a little more concerned. And I'm sure there were times when he felt he had the stuff to be there.

Gardner was the first of several outstanding veteran pitchers hidden out there in rural Nebraska that I would come in contact with, who for reasons hard for some to understand preferred their lives country-quiet and away from the routine demands of pro ball. There was no doubt in my mind, after watching and facing these pitchers, that they had the stuff to be there at some pro level, had they so desired.

Big husky Eddie McCarthy, a converted catcher, was the other half of the power duo secured for 1948 duty by the McCook Baseball Board. It had been noted that while catching, Eddie routinely threw the ball back to the mound with more velocity than it had had coming from the mound, no matter who was pitching, so they decided to put him out there on it. With blazing speed, big Ed had great success that year with McCook. He had been the ace pitcher for the Hastings Sultans, 1947 NIL champs; both he and Al McElreath had been financially enticed away from the angry Sultans to play for the Cats.

Designated Drivers and Sinking Spells

The NIL teams traveled by car to all away games. Players were not required to take their own cars but could do so if they found riding with the designated drivers too terrifying. The basic requirements for designated driver seemed to be a big powerful car and a heavy foot on the accelerator. Frightening as it was at times, having someone else do the driving after a long, hot night ball game was usually worth the tradeoff.

Midway through one of the trips, "Doc" Dennis, one of the regular designated drivers, suddenly pulled his big Buick onto the shoulder. "Give me a beer, Mildred," he said to his wife. "I'm having another one of my sinking spells."

Sinking spells? I thought. Yes, by all means have a beer if you are having sinking spells. Even consider changing drivers. I'm sure we have some volunteers back here. But Doc drank the beer and roared on down the road, as we slumped just a little deeper into the back seat and covered our eyes.

Reading Burma Shave signs with their clever verses and looking for white horses (a guaranteed base hit that night) were two traditional though not very challenging ways of passing time on the road.

The average trip was sixty or seventy miles—though Superior, Hastings, and Grand Island were considerably farther away. One of the regular designated drivers was Big Bill Hanke, who weighed about 270 and leaned back in the seat of his 1947 Hudson Hornet with his foot pushed to the floorboard from start to finish of each

Eddie Miller

trip. Grogan, a very intelligent engineering student, could not watch as Big Bill sped along the rural roads like an oversized bullet, ignoring the fact that automobile engineering advancement had long ago passed road safety standards and not seeming to care. Grogan would slump down out of sight between the seats and force himself to go to sleep, not opening his eyes until we stopped at the restaurant to eat before the game. I am certain this took twenty or thirty points off his batting average on some road trips.

High-speed driving, however, was not the most serious threat on the narrow two-lane highways. The real danger was from the senior citizen farmer in his slow car, creeping out from side roads onto faster roads. Since there was never much traffic on these small farm roads, the rural attitude toward collision was sometimes less than attentive. It even took the form of strange lapses from reality, as displayed by one local driver who honked the horn of his Model A Ford whenever he approached a railroad crossing.

During one trip to Holdrege we were about a third of a mile behind Big Bill Hanke when suddenly a big cloud of dust rolled up from the spot where his car had been. Completely shaken, we braked and slowed down, convinced we would find an overturned and smashed car or two as we peered through the settling trail of dust. To our breathless relief, we could see nothing but more dust as we worked our way forward in the low visibility. Then we suddenly came upon a huge, slow moving semitrailer truck just ahead of us, and after following it until the dust cleared enough to see down the highway, we passed it. Convinced that Big Bill's car was not demolished somewhere at the side of the road, we increased our speed and continued on to Holdrege. It wasn't long before we picked up the distinctive shape of the big Hudson Hornet far ahead of us, and we all cheered.

At the restaurant in Holdrege where we had planned to eat a meal before the game, we heard the story of what had happened. "This big semi just pulled out from the left onto the highway in front of us," Grogan said calmly. "I don't think he ever saw us. He was suddenly in our lane, with his trailer dragging across the other lane, so we couldn't go around him, even if it had been clear. Big Bill was going so fast he couldn't stop in time, so the only thing we could do was go off the road on the right side. We were lucky as hell there weren't any Burma Shave signs or culverts. We bounced all over the shoulder, and somehow Bill got us back on the highway beyond the truck, without rolling over a few times."

I was amazed at how calm Grogan was, since he, of all people, had been the most fearful of something like this. We ate supper, somehow able to swallow our food, and sat around for a while before suiting up slowly for the game. The players from Big Bill's car were especially quiet and pensive.

It wasn't until Bob Grogan went up to the plate before the game for batting practice that the effect of the experience really hit him. He started shaking so hard that he couldn't even hold on to the bat. His knees were so weak he had to go over and sit on the bench. He stayed there until we took infield practice.

The most hated trip in 1948, even though it was not the longest, was the one from McCook to North Platte. After the first eight miles we riders were sentenced to sixty miles of unrelenting, billowing gravel dust, and it was almost impossible to lag far enough back to allow it to settle and return the air to a tolerable breathing mixture and minimum safety visibility. There was understandably strong competition for occupancy in the first car. The moderate length of this trip was all that made it humanly acceptable. Had it been much longer, our physical fitness would have been compromised, and hazard pay might have been demanded. (The following year the remainder of the road was blacktopped, and NIL lung problems declined measurably.)

Apparently there was some difficulty assembling all of the regular designated drivers before one road trip to North Platte, because Grogan and I found ourselves assigned to a maroon 1947 Ford sedan and a new driver. Neither of us knew this polite, quiet man of about forty, and I cannot remember his name, but I was pleased and relieved that he drove with less speed and reckless abandon than some of the regulars did. Our trip to and from North Platte, though clogged with the usual billowing gravel dust, was quiet and relaxed, and Grogan seemed more reassured that we would reach our destination in one piece.

After we returned home, Eddie Miller, who had ridden in another car, met us with his friendly grin, this time accompanied with a sparkle in his eye. "How did the trip go, Bob?" Eddie asked Grogan, well aware of Bob's fear of flying on roads.

"Okay, I guess, why?" Bob said.

"Oh, I just wondered," Eddie said. "Did that little Ford go too fast for you?"

"No, we had a nice relaxed trip. Not too fast, for a change," Bob replied.

"So, you liked the new driver?"

"Well, yeah. He didn't say much at all. I was able to catch a little sleep instead of hiding on the floor. Why all the questions?"

"Oh, no reason," Eddie said. "I agree, for a guy with an artificial right leg, he drives pretty good, doesn't he?"

Grogan stared at Miller but said nothing. What Eddie had said was found to be true, and I was glad he'd waited until after the game to tell Bob. I don't think Spider would have had his three for four at the plate if he had known about it before the game.

Jeffers Field in North Platte was stuck down below and just to the west of the Jeffers Avenue overpass, the grandstand and playing field only fifteen or twenty yards north of the railroad tracks. Most NIL games were at night, so there was little annoyance from train action during the games, but because of this location Jeffers diamond boasted, or confessed to, a special blend of old switch-engine sifted cinders and black smokestack ashes over a deep layer of original Platte River silt and Sand Hills formula. Small wonder the infield appeared blacker than normal and muddy even when it wasn't.

Dragging the infield wasn't always such a good idea, since at times sharp cinder chunks would be turned up, and the expected "strawberries" from sliding increased to serious battle wounds. Also, diving for line drives in the infield was a last resort option for obvious reasons of chin and elbow skin care. How these larger cinders traveled from the switch engines' smokestacks to deep infield and even outfield locations was an intriguing aeronautical mystery. One thing was certain: the infield composition was constantly changing, depending on switch-engine activity, and fielding a hot ground ball would leave you feeling momentarily grateful if it found the pocket of your glove.

The North Platte Plainsmen of 1948 fielded Whitey Kurkowski, Bob Paulsen, Butch Nieman, Paul Ward, Lefty Mazell, Bailar, Extrum, Barraclough, and McCowin. Like those in Superior and Holdrege, very few of these players would still be in the lineup two years later. Only Paul Ward, deceptively swift hometown center fielder, and "Butch" Nieman would hold their own as drastic personnel turnovers continued to sweep through the NIL. We McCook Cats seemed to handle the Plainsmen with relative ease as the 1948 season unfolded. But just three years down the road the strength of the team from Buffalo Bill Cody's hometown presented a far different picture.

As we sped along the road to Kearney, a trip of about ninety-five miles, I shut my eyes and tried to doze off. I was not interested in looking for white horses anymore—I felt I could get my own base hits—and the familiar Burma Shave signs no longer commanded a watchful eye. We were headed for the biggest town in the league (that year) for a night ball game with a team which, I observed, created seriousness and resolve among the hometown McCook players. I had yet to feel anything like this. I had heard about but felt none of the tension that past conflicts had created for the locals; I was still wearing an inner smile at just the realization that I was playing baseball and getting a regular check for it. Baseball was to me at that time, and would remain, a game of innocent fun and exciting challenge—until "the Grand Island Incident."

The cause of most of this seriousness and resolve seemed to be a forty-year-old pitcher reverently referred to as Unca' Walt Ibsen, who this season was pitching for Kearney. Two decades earlier, on the front page of the *Holdrege Citizen* of May 24, 1928, the following account had appeared: "Walt Ibsen, rookie pitcher, turned back

Bertrand last Sunday on the Holdrege diamond 10 to 6 and he had a world of speed and curves with which to baffle the visitors."

Though it was hard for me to take seriously any pitcher called "Unca' Walt," if I had had that information when I first faced Ibsen, I would have calculated that I was all of two years old when "rookie" Walt pitched that game against Bertrand and known that I was now facing a pitcher with significant experience—twenty years, about ten of them in the NIL. Twenty-one years after that game with Bertrand, Ibsen struck out sixteen Lexington batters in a 2–0 NIL shutout to stake his claim as longevity champ of the league. During the years between, he had pitched for a number of towns throughout the area but had become a beloved and legendary part of Holdrege baseball lore.

Had I known all this in my first year in the NIL, I would have more fully appreciated and understood my difficulties in confronting this brooding moundsman with the Sal Maglie–like face. I would have realized that this was what real pitching was all about—control, surprise, keeping the hitter off balance with changes of speed and a good knuckle ball, showing a pitch that looked good to hit but suddenly— after you had decided to go after it—was not, and once in a while a sneaky fast ball you didn't know he still had. I would have fully understood why, though he looked hittable, my batting average kept falling when he was on the mound.

Kearney not only was the largest town in the league in 1948 (Hastings and Grand Island, each having brief visits in the NIL, were larger) but also had the most unusual ballpark. Built at the base of a hill, the diamond was surrounded by a semicircle of seats of solid concrete, much like an amphitheater. The seats were, of course, hard and uncomfortable, but they were cool in the hot summer nights. The Kearney Irishmen, with a number of veteran players, had been in the top division of the NIL for many years.

As we walked from our cars parked on a nearly level area about first-balcony height above the diamond, I heard that explosive crack of wood against horsehide over tightly wound wool yarn which always signaled a baseball struck with uncommon force. We walked to our dugout, but my eyes were on the batting cage to see who was responsible for that sound. Crack! Once more it reverberated through the still night air. A stocky right-handed hitter smiled and adjusted his cap as he admired the ball's rapid exit from the infield into the black night sky.

"Don't tell me they all hit like that up here," I muttered to Eddie Miller, who had seen what Kearney had put on the field for a number of years.

"No, not quite," Eddie said. "That's Floyd Stickney. He's the hardest-hitting third baseman in the league." As my brother Don—who later played with Stickney at Kearney—put it in a 1997 appraisal, Floyd was the last guy you wanted to see at the plate if you played third, which Don did. Stickney was typical of the talent that NIL teams were acquiring—former outstanding minor leaguers, drifting from here to there, who could still hit and field even if they had lost a step.

Floyd had been with Worthington in the old Western League in 1940, with Albany in the Georgia-Florida League in 1941, and with Mobile and Decatur, Illinois, in 1942. In 1946, before the "arms race" started, Stickney had won the NIL batting championship with the highest average in league history, a blistering .497 for the Kearney Irishmen.

When Kearney began infield practice, I watched two more veteran infielders smoothly turn the double play with the effortless moves of players who had done it many times before. Shortstop Del Harris and second baseman Gerald Peterson, both in their mid-thirties, would be up near the top of the NIL every year in batting average. After I watched them perform, I thought again, "I could play out here for a long time."

I remember the first trip to the very small town of Superior for several reasons. To begin with, it was a very long drive for a ball game—about 160 miles each way—and I wondered why Superior was even in this league, since it was so far from everybody. Among other reasons I remember this trip well was an incident that happened before the game.

We had suited up in a small dressing room by a swimming pool, and I was in full uniform except for my right shoe and sock. I wanted to tape my ankle, which I had turned a few days before, and since there wasn't convenient space inside, I stepped outside the small building and sat on the concrete step. I had begun putting strips of adhesive tape under my heel and over my arch—the way I had seen Buck Barger, our Nebraska U. trainer, do it—when an old gray sedan drove slowly by and came almost to a stop. On the passenger side the pinched face of an elderly lady with thick glasses appeared; her head and part of her upper body lurched through the open window as she indignantly exclaimed, "You ought to be ashamed of yourself!" Then the car picked up speed and drove away.

I looked up and around to see who she was talking to, but I was the only one out there. I quickly reviewed what had just happened and got to my feet.

"For what?" I shouted down the street as the car turned the corner. "What are you talking about, lady?" I checked my pants; they were buttoned up, as was my shirt. My uniform was complete to my cap except for one liner sock, one outer sock, and one shoe. What did this old "town decency" vigilante think she had seen? Was she representative of the town's knee-jerk suspicion of foreign, uncivilized baseball bums? Was there an ordinance forbidding outside ankle taping? I tried to dismiss the ludicrous incident as we drove to the ballpark. In those days, though, I thought I had to make everything fit, to find a reasonable answer to what I eventually saw as just a nutty old lady with longstanding sexual fears, fantasies, and frustrations.

At the ballpark I felt a warmer reception just from its coziness. Tall cottonwood trees surrounded the playing field, and others guarded the bleachers. The infield was smooth, its dark soil composition not good for rapid drying after a rain but baseball-inviting when accented with white bases and chalked baselines. The outfield grass was rich and smooth. It was the kind of park I enjoyed playing in, sheltered by trees from the wind and dust and allowing the game's familiar sounds to be heard clearly.

Standing out from the rest of the Superior team that year was a tall, lean first baseman who hit and threw right-handed. With a western hat on, he might have been mistaken for the town marshal. He moved around first base with a quickness and ease that told me immediately he had played some very high-level baseball before— with San Francisco in the Triple-A Pacific Coast League, I would learn. His name was Kermit Lewis, and after seeing him hit I understood why sportswriters often referred to him as "King Kermit." This lean but muscular thirty-nine-year-old with incredibly fast wrists and hands would wait on a pitch, his bat vertical and perfectly still, and yet still whip the bat head out in time to pull the ball high over the left-field fence. His outstanding bat speed, which exploded late on a pitch, gave him time to see the breaking ball. They did not fool Kermit with the curve, and very few could get the fast ball by him. He also had surprising running speed, getting down to first faster than many players half his age, even though he always complained that his feet hurt. Lewis would play not only for Superior but also for Holdrege and North Platte, becoming a huge winning force for all three teams.

It wasn't until we all sat on our bench that I noticed a flaw in this classic small-town hardball setting. The park's architect had designed the bleachers a little close to the fence just behind our bench, and the effect was of far too many people on our bench for one ball team.

"Hey, four-eyes!" The voice came from just behind my shoulder. "Wait until you try to hit Jake Bornschlegl! You'll need six eyes!" I felt a sudden damp sprinkle on my neck, but the sky was clear. I ignored the comment and the sprinkle. It was basic baseball wisdom never to acknowledge the heckling fan. If you did, you would be the target for the remainder of the game, and your name would be "Rabbit Ears" because you heard so well.

"Yeah, four-eyes!" another voice said. He was going to say something else but couldn't think of anything.

"You'll need eight eyes," a third voice added. The distinct aroma of beer cast a tavernlike atmosphere over our bench. We looked for the umpires to call for the lineups and get this game going.

"Who's pitching for the McCook 'Pussy Cats' tonight?" voice number one demanded.

"Felix!" voice number two quickly answered. The first two rows of bleachers directly behind me convulsed in laughter, and I secretly hoped they would break down.

"Krazy," an unidentified voice said. "Krazy Kat."

"No, it's 'Baldy' Garland," voice number three corrected, unintentionally belching on the word "Baldy." He was referring to Dave Garland, a twenty-eight-year-old pitching ace out of Denver who had played for several NIL teams besides McCook and who was prematurely losing hair to male-pattern baldness. At Superior, Dave had once unfortunately taken off his cap to wipe away the sweat.

"Where is Baldy," number one said, noticing he was not on the bench, "getting a head shine?" The faithful cackled again at this one.

"And where is Turkey Neck Skoog?" number three said.

"Hey, four-eyes!" voice number two shouted. "Wake up! You haven't said much lately! Would you like us to wake you up when the game starts?" Bill Gardner and P. O. Karthauser walked twenty yards away from the bench down the right-field line and began warming up.

"There's Felix warming up now," voice number one said. "Hey, Felix! Felix the Cat!"

Gene Dellenbach, fine glove man at first base who also wore glasses, picked up a couple of bats and walked down the fence toward right field to loosen up his swing and to get some quiet time.

"Hey!" a new voice called out. "There's another four-eyes!"

"You! Four-eyes number two!" voice number one said. "Home plate is over there."

When Whitey Skoog signaled time to take infield practice, our team rose as one man and trotted eagerly to our positions.

"There's Turkey Neck," voice number two said. "I thought he fell asleep too and missed the trip."

This section of the Superior diamond was the exact location where, a couple of years later, McCook's smooth-fielding first baseman Jack Baxter would put on an original clinic of crowd control, the equal of which I have never seen. After listening to and tiring of a similar chorus of personal criticism of our appearance and ability from the bleacher jockies, Jack suddenly stood up and slowly turned to face the critics—thereby, we thought, dooming himself with the dreaded rabbit-ears label for the rest of the game.

Baxter tilted his head back and raised his first finger to get their full attention. Looking like a spinster schoolteacher peering down her nose at a group of small children who were misbehaving, Jack said, "No-o-o-o-oh." The word was soft and high-pitched but firm, as he held his pose. For a few seconds all was silent. The hecklers, momentarily disoriented by this strange response from our bench, forgot their project. Then they remembered and rallied. Baxter quickly issued a second, slightly sterner "No-o-o-OH," stunning them again. After trying several more times and being met with the same prompt correction, the Superior bench jockeys became completely disorganized and tried spitting down between their feet and lighting cigarettes to regain their poise. Every time an abuser would try a sneak attack, Baxter would halt him with a corrective finger and form a silent, "No-o-o-oh" with his lips. Soon the momentum the Superiorites had felt certain would steamroll over the helpless Cats was completely dissipated, and the hecklers were lighting second cigarettes before the first ones had been discarded. None of us would ever see a hostile group of fans so effectively confused and quieted at the old ball game.

The night of my first game there, Superior fielded the team of De-Lozier, Stewart, Taylor, Somerhalder, McLaughlin, Maul, Koch, Kubat, and Bornschlegl. I list these names because two years later none of them would be in the lineup. The NIL was just beginning to see an astonishing change in personnel. Young Superior was no powerhouse in 1948; the same would not be said of the strong team assembled by 1950. Superior, unlike the on-and-off Hastings team, had come to play and stay. The lineup that night was just a working beginning.

The Left-Handed Legend
of Lexington and
Other Moundsmen

For a long time—since about 1936 or before—all Elmer "Lefty" Haines had to do was toss his glove out on the mound, and local sports reporters would begin writing of another Lexington victory. It didn't matter who the team was, the legend tells; Lefty could beat them. The book on Lefty was that he had just too much "country" in him to leave the farm and was too shy for the city life of pro ball. No one will ever know whether he could have pitched in the majors. They do know he beat just about everybody around western Nebraska for a couple of decades. Lefty always pitched at home, and I don't think it was just because of the lights (although I once momentarily lost a ground ball deep in the hole between first and second on a muddy night at Lexington). It was more that if Lexington fans had come to the game and found someone else on the mound, they might have become confused and left for home, thinking they were in the wrong park.

We dressed in all kinds of places on road trips—schoolhouses, auditoriums, city halls, swimming pools, armories, bathhouses, jailhouses, hotels, and motels. My first time in Lexington we were assigned to the city hall. It also turned out to be the city jail, and we were to suit up in the room to the south of the chief of police's office.

Just before we learned that, a police cruiser wheeled up swiftly and braked in a cloud of dust. One of the officers jumped out and dashed inside; he opened a desk drawer in the chief's office and excitedly fumbled for some keys. Then he hurried back outside to herd two noisy citizens out of the cruiser and into the city hall/jail, push-

Lefty Haines

ing one of them into the empty cell right next to where we were standing. The officer snapped the lock on the cell door, and the prisoner spoke.

"You ain't going to lock me in no jail, you prick!" he shouted at the cop. I was certain he had failed the straight-line walking test.

"Where do we suit up?" P. O. Karthauser asked, unmoved by all the sudden commotion.

"Right in there," the cop said, happy to change the subject.

"You prick!" the prisoner said to Eddie Miller, who was watching events along with the rest of us.

"Me?!" Eddie said. "Why you shit! Let that guy out of there," Miller called to the officer, who, with the other citizen, had taken the keys and gone after bail. "I'll fix that prick," Ed shouted. "What does he call me names for? Why does that prick call me a prick?!"

"He's drunk," I said.

"I don't care," Eddie said, "I'll break him apart! Where's those keys?"

Behind Eddie's almost constant grin was one tough Cat, and the rowdy Lexington citizen would never know how close to real pain he came. We suited up, and somebody asked if we should take our valuables with us. The answer was, if they weren't safe in the police station, where would they be? We took them with us. Eddie shot one last look at the prisoner, who by then had passed out, and we went out to play ball. I expected Miller to take Lefty Haines deep a couple of times that night.

When we reached the ball field, I thought how appropriate the nickname "Minutemen" was for the Lexingtons. The red-brown snow fencing surrounding the outfield in the out-of-town setting gave one the feeling of playing pasture baseball in Revolutionary War days. Not that the infield wasn't well tended—the ball took reasonably true hops—and the outfield wasn't too rough, although Irv Coufal, Lexington center fielder, once fainted from being stung by large hornets that swarmed out from some kind of underground nest in the outfield. It was the long stretch of flat farmland behind the outfield fence that gave the park the early American feeling.

As the fans began to arrive, filling up the small grandstand behind home plate, the ball diamond began to seem more active and contemporary. A left-handed pitcher began warming up for Lexington as we took infield practice. He threw easily from a three-quarter motion, but the ball reached the catcher sooner than the motion indicated, releasing a crisp, leathery "snapping" sound. The catcher lobbed the ball back to the left-hander, who quickly and smoothly repeated the fluid action, everything in proper sequence, producing deceptively effortless arm speed with power and control. So that's the old left-hander, I thought, eyeing the strong, broad-shouldered wheat farmer who threw with the sophisticated ease of a Whitey Ford; so that's the Lefty Haines they have all been talking about. He looks like he knows what he's doing so far.

Haines began to heat up a little faster, and the catcher's mitt released louder sounds as this veteran left-hander, his baseball cap tilted noticeably to the left side, continued throwing with what appeared to be a mixture of boredom, cockiness, and well-earned confidence. He motioned "curve ball" to his catcher, and the pitch looked like it glanced off an invisible telephone pole just in front of the plate.

I don't remember exactly how I did against Haines that night. I do know, being a fast ball hitter and his fast ball having a lot of movement on it, he caught me looking a few times on pitches that slid back over the inside part of the plate for solid strikes. And one or two swings caught the pitch far out on the bat where the bees live, leaving my hands buzzing and me not anticipating a quick return. And I believe I struck out a couple of times—that night and others to follow. Lefty had my attention, and that game had my number.

About sixty miles due east of McCook was Holdrege, the shortest trip for the Cats in 1948. Holdrege, Lexington, and Superior were the "little" towns in the NIL that year; McCook was the middle-sized one; North Platte and Kearney were the "big" towns. During my first year Unca Walt Ibsen—pitcher of mythological duration and proportions who was identified, when all was written, with

Holdrege—was not pitching for the Holdrege Bears; it was the season he pitched for Kearney.

That year, however, the Bears did have big, rough Art Dollaghan. The young, hot-tempered, hard-throwing right-hander had impressive credentials of his own, such as having been NIL strikeout leader the year before. Art was an imposing figure on the mound and was indeed fast with excellent control—even when he threw at your head. But what made him still more valuable was his ability to hit with anyone in the league, and hit the long ball. He was usually in the middle of the lineup, sometimes even when he pitched. Defensively, he could play outfield or first, and his team suffered no reduction in defense when he did.

The Holdrege ballpark was just southeast of town, facing east with a grandstand view of forever beyond a chain-link outfield fence that cut across the farming flatness. The old wooden grandstand had a small announcing booth in the center, and in 1948 hearty Bob Morris, sportscaster for the McCook radio station, traveled to all road games and broadcast them back to radio-glued McCookers. The excitement and team following that year became infectious. After only a few games it was clear this was not the last-place Cats' club of 1946–47 anymore.

For some reason our bombastic catcher, P. O. Karthauser, forged a unique relationship with the Holdrege fans. They hated him. Or at least they pretended to, venting all their hostilities on his powerful shoulders. P. O. knew just how to kindle the sputtering sparks into bleacher bonfires by furiously disputing umpire calls that favored Holdrege, and now and then talking back to the bleacherites.

The 1948 Holdrege scorecard recorded the lineup of Marks, Rinehart, Hansen, Johnson, Quick, Strong, Bienoff, Majors, Charlesworth, Dollaghan, and Meisenbach. Many of these would be missing the following year as the Bears became the first NIL team to follow the McCook Cats' radical lead in substantial outside recruitment.

Notable among names in the foregoing lineup is Max Quick, a unique semi-pro package. Booked to play one position or another from one town to another, Max was probably the highest paid semi-pro player in Nebraska. Operating out of Stromsburg, this very solid, 190-pounder who topped six feet was first sought after for his pitching talents, which were outstanding. He was as fast as anyone in the state; and it would have taken a radar gun, which they didn't have in those days to measure a pitcher's speed, to determine if he was the fastest. After it was observed that he could hit with equal power and excellence, Max became a widely used outfielder when he needed arm rest between mound starts. He, like Dollaghan, could play both offense and defense and was at home in several positions. But Max would have been in great demand on the mound even if he "couldn't hit a lick," because he could win. I had hit against him when I played for Sandy's Goetz team against Stromsburg, and I played with him later in a few games at North Platte. He had a compact delivery like a catcher—something like Roger Clemens among modern high-profile pitchers. Max very possibly held the record for "most towns pitched for" in Nebraska.

Box Scores, Base Hits,
and Special Assignments

Facing east into the warm McCook morning sun was a strangely narrow two-story sandstone building on Main Street (now Norris Avenue). At the top of this building chiseled letters spelled out "19—Gazette—26." I always thought it was a special sign: the building that would be my happy place of summer employment for three years was built the year I was born.

It *was* a happy time. Of all the jobs I have had in my life, I can't remember any of them with more fondness than my time in the sunny eastern corner of the *Gazette* building. Each morning I would come to work with anticipation and excitement. The big Royal typewriter was there awaiting my highly charged imagination, influenced by William Saroyan, Damon Runyon, and Red Smith, to spring into action.

Down the hallway mild-tempered sports editor Les Spence waited patiently for my copy. There were always deadlines, but I never felt stressed. I had time to write, to create, to learn the craft of newspaper writing. I was not a journalism major—I had never even had a class in journalism—but I found writing more challenging and exciting than my art studies. I wasn't getting rich at the *Gazette* but I was very happy. If I had worn a necktie, I would have loosened it; a hat, I would have tilted it jauntily back on my head. Visualizing myself that way as the teletype machine pounded out faraway stories down the hall, I would begin my column.

The shadowy Harry Strunk made one of his rare appearances one morning in August 1948. Through the glass I caught the tall,

Harrry Strunk

bent form of my boss making his way toward his upstairs retreat. He paused at the doorway to my office. It wasn't really my office. I was one of three reporters who used the typewriters there.

"How is everything going?" the elusive owner of the *Gazette* asked me.

I straightened up and quickly began doing reporter things, like putting two thin sheets of copy paper in the typewriter. Cy Sherman had told me back at the *Lincoln Star* always to use two sheets—not three, not one—two sheets to make a proper cushion for the keys. I stopped looking like Red Smith for a moment, smiled, and gave the boss my full attention.

"Just fine, Mr. Strunk. Everything is just fine," I said.

Harry stood there for a moment, smiling and frowning at the same time as usual. Then he continued, "I have a special assignment for you. I want you to meet the train tomorrow. They're bringing home a soldier, and I want you to do a piece on it," he said.

A special assignment. A real reporter's assignment, not just sports stuff. I felt excited.

"Okay," I said. "When does the train come in?"

"Four o'clock," my boss said.

"Great," I said. "I'll be there." I had some questions, but I just nodded because I didn't want to show any ignorance of the business.

"In the morning," Mr. Strunk added, and turned back to the hallway.

The next morning shortly before 4:00 A.M. I sat in the dark at the station with a pencil and a pad and a terrible cup of coffee in a paper cup, waiting for the train to pull in. About five hours later I wrote the following piece, which appeared on the front page, lower left-hand corner, of the August 30, 1948, *McCook Gazette*:

There are things which go on during the night and early morning, that the sleeping people of a town never know.

A dead man moves quietly down Main Street in a long, black car at four in the morning, while a sleepy man on his way to work stands at attention and salutes.

Twenty-five American Legion and Veterans of Foreign

Wars members march beside that car in silent tribute to a guy who lost his life in recent warfare.

What's his name? What does it matter? He is one of the thousands who died overseas in the late world war, and is being brought home for the last time. The twenty-five men marching in "guard of honor" up Main street in McCook—yes, here in McCook—have climbed out of bed in the dark of night to pay tribute to one who might have been sleeping too, instead of lying motionless, had fate seen otherwise. They understand.

The guard of honor halts in front of the funeral home, where the body will remain a time. The United States, American Legion and VFW flags were carried in front of him from the station to the home.

He may have lived in McCook, or he may have lived in Culbertson. No difference. He was brought to this station in McCook, and those American Legion and VFW vets were there to see that he made it the rest of the way O.K. All twenty-five of them . . . at four A.M.

Twenty-five veterans go home . . . or to their jobs as a pink light begins to glow in the East . . . the sun comes up to wake the people of McCook . . . but the "visitor" will never waken.

As I learned more about McCook, I learned a bit more about Mr. Strunk as well. For example: Angling on a southeastern course down past Maywood, Curtis, Stockville, and Cambridge in southwestern Nebraska, Medicine Creek normally flowed innocently and predictably through the heart of NIL territory and south to the Republican River Drainage Basin, where the towns of Culbertson, McCook, Indianola, Bartley, Cambridge, Holbrook, Arapahoe, and Oxford lay in a west-to-east pattern. But after abnormally violent downpours, Medicine Creek could rapidly fill up and rush over its banks with deadly destruction. In 1935 a sudden flood killed 113 unsuspecting residents. A similar terrifying event left 13 dead as Medicine Creek waters swept through on the morning of June 22, 1947, just a year before I became a member of the McCook Cats.

For twelve years concerned local citizens had lobbied for changes to prevent future disasters, but until 1946 no flood-control construction had even begun in the entire valley. As the August 7, 1948, *McCook Gazette* noted in its Medicine Creek Dam dedication special, however, engineers and construction workers were by then well on their way to completing the third major dam in the Republican River Drainage Basin.

Since the 1935 disaster, the one man most responsible for pursuing efforts to control flooding in this area was my weathered newspaper-veteran boss, Harry D. Strunk, publisher of the *Gazette*. I learned this not from him or any of his family but from daily exposure to front-page stories and his editorials, and from conversation with civic-minded McCook residents. It was Harry who finally got the Bureau of Reclamation, the Army Corps of Engineers, the Department of Agriculture, and powerful individuals to break ground and begin actual physical projects to control future disasters in this vulnerable valley. His editorials and relentless pressure on state senators finally brought action through legislation. In recognition of his efforts, a small lake just north of Medicine Creek Dam was named Harry Strunk Lake. In that August 7, 1948, issue of the *Gazette*, Harry wrote,

We dedicate this edition to the pioneers, who on many occasions, before and since, have suffered the ravages of floods, drouth, hot winds, dust storms, tornadoes and depression.

It is with deepest respect and appreciation that we set aside a portion of this edition in recognition of the part the Bureau of Reclamation, the Army Engineers, the Department of Agriculture and other agencies have played and are playing in this work, to the end that such catastrophes MUST never occur again . . . that in their place MUST come security and prosperity.

Helping to survey territory for some of those Bureau of Reclamation projects in 1948 was McCook shortstop Bob Grogan, intelligent engineering student from the University of Nebraska. When Bob arrived at McCook in 1948, he had immediately been employed by the bureau as a surveyor at a very good salary.

"You have to wear thick, high-top boots and be on the lookout for rattlesnakes all the time," Bob said, lugging his triangulating equipment through the windblown prairie grass east of McCook. Considering the long, hot hours on his feet out there surveying, even on the day of league games, Bob played exceptional baseball for the McCook Cats, still able to "work the web" at shortstop, like the "Spider" he had been nicknamed, and smash long extra-base hits into the outfield gaps. Doc Dennis and Pat Patrick must have talked the bureau's bosses into letting Spider off work a little early to get some rest before those crucial games at the end of the NIL pennant chase. I appreciated the luxury of working inside the comparatively cool *Gazette* building with a ceiling fan circulating the air. It was one of the perks in a job which, compared to Grogan's high-demand, high-paying survey work, had little going for it in the way of salary.

Writing for the local paper, though, sometimes meant sharing the town's grief as well as its games. In a town the size of McCook the death of any town resident brought sadness to family, friends, and neighbors. When it was the death of a popular young high school student and promising athlete, it brought sorrow to the whole school and many townspeople as well. And if it was an accidental death, a needless tragedy, it brought not only grief to the town but also shock.

Such an accidental death occurred shortly after I began my job as sportswriter and reporter at the *McCook Gazette*. The tragedy was reported on the front page when it happened, and months later I wrote of how the student friends of sixteen-year-old Ted Sloniker, promising football player and citizen, refused to let his memory be forgotten. In my "Sports Haze" column of the June 16, 1949, issue of the *Gazette* the following story appeared:

A tall, red-headed center finished football practice one evening almost a year ago, and good naturedly jumped into a "dog pile" before going in to shower.

to see this new thing called "winning." (Unfortunately, whereas the little Eastside diamond was in very fine condition, the new larger park—named Fairgrounds Ballpark because it was where they had formerly held an annual rodeo and fair—was not; we sometimes thought the infield had not been dragged since the last Brahma bull–riding contest.) The five-player overhaul of the McCook Cats represented the kind of single-minded town purpose which would soon hit every town in the league, and the shock waves would shake the financial foundations of them all. From some sportswriters came angry cries of "foul" and "gloom and doom and destruction" for the NIL. Not surprisingly, most of the criticism came from the towns struggling to keep up in this new fast-lane baseball league.

So intense did the competition and financial anxiety become in 1949 as the playoff selections were being decided that angry arguments and even fistfights erupted in a few of the hot evening battles, creating tenseness and ugly moods among the towns and resulting in protests being filed and suspensions handed out. This was the season when Floyd Stickney, league president, suspended North Platte's ace catcher, Bob Paulson, for losing control and knocking out umpire Ed Manley. Then the embarrassed Stickney had to level the same penalty on himself a few weeks later, when he couldn't keep his own emotions in check and punched out Grand Island shortstop Jerry Koch during a hot argument over a play at home plate. Things became very tense over the prospect of losing out on the playoff gate money.

As for me, I generally enjoyed the league games as an interested but basically neutral visitor who periodically went up to hit and out to field my position. In 1948 I appreciated the lack of emotional involvement that gave me the freedom to play relaxed baseball. This serenity would not last forever. In 1949 I would be drawn into some personal involvement and conflict, like it or not.

Bob West

Baseball or a College Education—or Both?

The late September skies began to change shades of blue and the lazily drifting white cumulus clouds of summer eased higher and thinner, sketching light cirrus patterns, announcing the end of baseball for that year and the coming of Cornhusker football.

The football program at Nebraska in 1948 was struggling through a short period of serious rebuilding. After thrilling the fans in 1941 by going to the Rose Bowl and giving Frankie Albert and the Stanford T formation a scare in the first half, the Huskers emerged from the war years with a run of average coaches and teams. Only a few outstanding players—Tom Novak, Charlie Toogood, Cletus Fischer, Dick Hutton, Carl Samuelson, Ralph Damkroger, and Joe Partington—showed individual flashes of the greatness of the notable teams of the 1930s and very early 1940s, when all-Americans George Sauer, Charlie Brock, and Sam Francis plus such other outstanding players as Lloyd Cardwell, "Vike" Francis, Herm Rohrig, Ed and Sam Swartzkopf, Johnny Howell, and Elmer Dohrman filled the pages of my big junior high scrapbook. I remember listening to one game in which center Charlie Brock made four consecutive tackles on a thrilling and successful goal-line stand.

When you entered the football stadium, back when the field had rich green grass (no reflective milky-green shimmer of sun on Astroturf in those days) and held only about thirty-nine thousand fans, the sights and sound were breathtaking. Punters boomed the football into high, echoing spirals, and quarterbacks fired long passes to crisscrossing receivers. Nebraska players raced about in bursts of speed, their white helmets, brilliant red jerseys with huge white block numerals, and gold pants (they were gold satin then) colorful against the deep green of the grass. This image still remains in my mind from the sunny but cold day in 1936 when I was ten years old, and my dad took me to my first Nebraska game. I saw left-footed all-American fullback Sam Francis, with no wind to assist him, punt far over the safety man's head at the fifty-yard line—the ball finally rolling dead on the eight-yard line after eighty-seven yards of flight—and roll on the grass, to the delight and amazement of the roaring capacity crowd. I saw Lloyd Cardwell, the "wild horse," gallop the length of the field for a touchdown on a kickoff, and my feet got very cold. It was a wonderful day.

Some people believe that trying to be a college athlete and serious student at the same time just will not work, that any attempt to resolve the built-in problems and hazards can only compromise educational or artistic standards. In my undergraduate experience there were two professors who surprised me with this fixed opinion, which I considered narrow-minded and selfish. Their stated reasons differed, but both had the same purpose: to remind students how important their own subjects were. "Trivial" activities unrelated to the crucial value of the courses they taught could not be allowed to detract from such serious work.

Albin T. Anderson taught history at the University of Nebraska. He was a regal blond Swede, standing a lean six-foot-four, with sharply chiseled features and pale blue eyes. When Albin T. lectured to the overflowing class of more than a hundred students, my mind drifted and I saw him in an Ingmar Bergman film, walking the shore and staring out into the sea. My mind would come back from the Bergman sea long enough to hear, and long remember, the "family Hohenzollern," which took up one whole lecture period of European history. Albin T. Anderson was an intimidating, self-possessed lecturer. The emotional distance between him and the tightly packed roomful of dutiful note-takers was noticeable and not accidental. Albin T. spoke; we took notes. There was never any discussion. Impeccable in his white shirt, tie, tan herringbone wool sport coat, and charcoal brown wool slacks, Professor Anderson droned on in his measured baritone through a scripted lecture timed to end exactly one minute and thirty-five seconds after the class bell. He then stacked his papers, put them in his leather attaché case, and strode to his office, leaving his students fumbling with their stacks of books, not daring to approach him with questions.

When there was a quiz in Professor Anderson's class, a teaching assistant monitored the activities; Albin T. would not even be there. One such quiz was scheduled for the day we also had a ball game with Minnesota University. It was not a conference game but a "bragging rights" game between the Big Ten and the Big Seven. I made an appointment to speak of this with my distant professor of history, who sat behind a large mahogany desk stacked with important papers and books.

"Yes," he said, in a voice I was certain would be followed by a glance at his watch.

"I'm starting second baseman for the university baseball team," I began softly, "and we have a game Tuesday afternoon. As you know, that is also a quiz day for the class."

Professor Anderson leaned back in his cushioned swivel chair and nodded slowly.

"Go on," he said.

"I would like to ask you if I can make up this quiz later. I'll come in any time to do it. The game is important, and I am important to the team, but I also know these quizzes count 20 percent of my grade, and I am very concerned about my academic average," I explained.

Anderson studied me for a moment, but only a moment.

"You've got to make up your mind whether you're in college to get an education or to play baseball. The decision is yours," he said flatly.

I had expected something like this but was still surprised by the cold and inflexible answer, and how quickly he gave it.

"I would like to do both," I said.

Anderson stood up in his Bergmanesque stiffness, walked to the window, and stared out, scanning the icy waters of his academic rigidity.

"Well, I can't let you make up the quiz," he said, still staring out the window. "I do not have a makeup policy. If I did, everyone would try to buy extra time, and the scheduling would be in chaos." He looked at me for a moment and then sat down with his papers. "You'll just have to suffer the consequences in your grade if you choose to play a baseball game instead of coming to class," he concluded.

I had never actually had any feelings toward Albin T. Anderson before, but at that moment I felt like knocking all his books and papers clear across the room. I didn't, of course. "Thank you for your time," I said. I turned slowly and left through the heavy office door, holding back my true feelings.

I played in the Minnesota game and also passed the course with a final grade of 82.

Sometime later—I've forgotten just when—the Anderson mystique led some to believe he should run for governor of Nebraska. During the debates his cold remoteness came across, and though it did not matter to the note-taking students in his bulging classes, apparently it did to the voters, for he was unsuccessful in his bid for office. I didn't usually take pleasure in the defeats of others, but this time I made an exception. I imagined meeting Professor Anderson on campus and, after identifying myself, saying, "You know, Albin, you have to decide whether you're here to teach and advise students, or to play politics."

The second professor was Kady Faulkner, "Mother Art" in Nebraska's art department for many years before Duard Laging and his "new movement" group slipped into Morrill Hall and flushed her out of her nest in 1949. Kady was a gray-haired woman in a gray flannel skirt suit. Her face was carved with a perpetual smile that conveyed not amusement or happiness but a self-designed expression of fifty years of wisdom about to be imparted. Her wrinkled forehead above her rimless glasses told of many deep "impartings" over the decades, and she always had at her feet a circle of devoted followers.

Kady talked of painting with a unique intensity. There were certain pigments which, especially when applied with a palette knife, would cause her to rhapsodize to the extent that she once actually spoke of having the urge to eat the paint right off the knife; I believe it was alizarin crimson. I think some of us wondered if we would come to class one day and find her absent and in the emergency room from an overdose of Grumbacher oils.

At the drawing bench one day Kady stopped to look at my work. She discussed my drawing and then—maybe because I was wearing my red letter sweater with a big white "N" on my chest—surprised me by saying, "You know, you'll have to choose between being a baseball player and being an artist. You can't do both."

I looked at her a moment and then, realizing she was serious, said, "Of course I can. Why not?"

"Your hands are very important to you as an artist. You could easily break the fingers of your painting hand playing baseball. Then what would you do?"

I thought a moment.

"I'd paint left-handed," I said. "I would just practice until I could control my left hand well. You yourself have said you draw and paint with knowledge. It would just be a matter of slowly learning how to direct the left hand as I do the right," I continued, believing I had made a very good point. Kady stared at me, her wrinkled forehead becoming more compressed as her eyebrows pushed down from the outsides. Her masklike smile seemed to search for words, not necessarily ones of wisdom.

"You can't do both," she repeated, finally, as if her saying it made it true, and walked on to enlighten the next student.

I had occasion to remember this conversaton when I was teaching at Kansas State University in 1952. I had visited the art department at Nebraska U. after my first summer with the North Platte Plainsmen and had asked Duard Laging, then department chairman, if by any chance he had any teaching openings. Duard shook his head.

"However," he said, "we just received this announcement today of a teaching position opening at Kansas State. We haven't even put it on the bulletin board yet." He reached into his desk and handed me the job description.

"This says, 'in the Engineering Department,'" I noted. "I can't teach engineering classes."

"Read on," Chairman Laging said. "The job is to teach drawing, design, and painting to architecture students. At Kansas State the art department seems to be split into two factions: one in the architecture department, which is inside the engineering department, and another in the home economics department, which is focused on fashion drawing and related courses."

"So, I would be teaching art subjects to architecture students, not home economics students?" That was the way Duard understood it.

I applied immediately for the position and was interviewed and hired. A few weeks later one of my life drawing students from New Jersey came to class with a cast on his right hand.

"I can't draw for a while," he said, trying to appear disappointed. "I broke my wrist."

"Sure you can, Howie," I said, recalling my dialogue with Kady Faulkner three years before. "You can draw left-handed."

"How can I? I'm right-handed," Howie answered.

"So am I. Put your tablet up on the easel and give me some charcoal," I continued. I took the charcoal in my left hand and studied the standing model for a moment.

"Howie," I began, "I know from previous observation from all sides that this girl's head fits into her neck like this, and the neck into the torso like this, and the weight on her right leg causes the spine to swing like this, and the right hip joint is higher than the left like this." I sketched light, thoughtful strokes with the charcoal, building an armature around which to add some flesh. In a few moments there was some volume to accent with heavier lines, and to my own surprise, I had a crude drawing with more expression and character than some of the right-handed drawings I had turned out in a repetitious, slick manner. My lack of easy facility had made me review closely what I knew.

"See," I said, "you draw from knowledge, and the lack of immediate hand control makes you look closer and observe more. You get better as you think and study the model, while gradually gaining control of your left hand."

I added a few more heavy accents, feeling the relaxed fun of entering new territory and, in case I failed, having an excuse to offer those who expected greatness from me. Feeling that I was on a roll, I created some volume with uncharacteristic abandon, realizing I had just come through on the spot, proving my untested theory to Howie and a few other students who had gathered, and teaching myself that to dare to try is what life is all about. I handed the charcoal to Howie, whose eyes were wider than before.

"Now you try one," I said. "Go slowly at first, keep it light, look and think. If you are not sure, go up and take a closer look." (I'd had a sculpture instructor at the Chicago Art Institute who would say, "Go up and touch her, if you're not sure." But I wasn't going to suggest anything nearly that familiar, even though the Kansas State 1952 dress code for art models was a one-piece bathing suit.)

Howie began furtively, putting thoughtful strokes on the paper. To my amazement, within a week or two his left-handed drawings were more sensitive, accurate, and interesting than any of his earlier right-handed work. A beginning student, trusting me completely, had proved the spur-of-the-moment theory, one I had advanced three years before in rebuttal to the belief of the lady in the gray flannel suit that I had to choose between art and baseball. Howie was as delighted as I was; in fact, he kept proudly drawing left-handed even after the cast came off. I almost switched hands myself, having rediscovered the search-and-discover aspect of the drawing process.

I liked my rich red letter sweater with the big white "N" on the chest; I was proud of being in the N-Club with the other top athletes at the university, especially the football lettermen. Strangely enough, though, I felt self-conscious wearing it, because being naturally a nonjoiner and a solitary creative person, viewing much of life as a distant observer, I realized I was calling attention to myself. It made me uncomfortable, yet at the same time my desire to be recognized as someone with special abilities prompted me to wear it. I was also self-conscious in those days about wearing glasses and being an athlete. In the N-Club photograph very few of us wore glasses. I imagined other students passing by on campus thinking, "I don't recognize him at all. I wonder what sport he lettered in?"

I would almost smile and turn as they passed and say, "Baseball." But, of course this was all just in my mind, and I didn't say anything, because they weren't really paying any attention to me.

I was also a little uncomfortable about making it known on the baseball team that I was an art major. Some art students chose to behave in frivolous ways, flaunting their individuality and at times appearing immature and silly. To most athletes on campus, such behavior translated to their being "fruits" and "fairies." I was not eager to be included in this predetermined group, and though I didn't think of my fellow artmakers in just those terms, I did recognize that they often acted unlike N-Club material.

So it helped sustain me in those difficult times to find another big red sweater with a big "N" on it being worn by another art student in most of my classes. His name was Bill Moomey (some enviously called him "Golden Boy"), and he ran the 60-yard low hurdles and 60-yard dash in track, played some halfback for the football team, and married a very attractive sorority girl. Moomey could draw exceptionally well and could sing with equal excellence. He would break into a very good imitation of Vaughn Monroe's "Racing with the Moon" when Kady Faulkner stepped out of the room, quickly clearing up any doubts about his self-confidence or talent. His ease with making art and athletics compatible was helpful to me, and we got along just fine together.

Since I was drawing sports cartoons for the *Lincoln Star*, Bill, being an excellent draftsman himself, began doing some sports and fashion drawings for the *Lincoln Journal*. We carried on a friendly competition for best N-Club newspaper artist in the department. I think it helped both of us to have athletic company throughout our art studies, and Kady Faulkner spoke no more to me about the incompatibility of art and sports.

That spring the 1949 Nebraska baseball team, stimulated by our startling Big Seven championship in 1948, intended to continue its impressive success. But despite the addition of Tom Novak, all-American football great and excellent all-round catcher, who would hit .351 that year, our team did not win the close ones and were not so successful in the standings. This would prove to be a year to re-group for another run at the crown in 1950.

George Gribble

Nebraska's Other
Semi-Pro Leagues

Geographically, the Nebraska Independent League was a south-western Nebraska league. North Platte, the team farthest north, was still in the southern half of the state. Superior was the one exception, being 160 miles east of McCook and almost out of the state on the southern border. It would have made more sense from a location standpoint for Superior to be in the Cornhusker League. I'm not clear how or why this team got started in the NIL, but I did notice during my playing years that Superior was willing to sacrifice the town's financial resources to stay and compete in that free-wheeling, fast-lane league.

In northeastern Nebraska the Pioneer Nite League functioned in a cluster of towns north and a little west of the state capital, Lincoln, and the largest city in the state, Omaha. The small towns of Pender, O'Neil, Wakefield, and Wayne were the farthest north and most remote from the two big cities. The league's competing used mostly hometown players plus some Lincoln and Omaha recruits.

In 1948 the PNL operated with a north and a south division and held a playoff at the end of the season. That year Fremont won three out of four games in the north-south playoff with Pender in what the Fremont newspaper account called the "hottest series in PNL history." George Gribble, Fremont shortstop, hit a remarkable .500 (9 for 18) for the series. In fact, Fremont was probably the strongest and most consistent winner, the team to beat in the PNL.

Throughout 1948 the PNL team batting orders remained fairly constant, with some roving exceptions, of course. As noted earlier, the much-sought-after Max Quick, fast ball ace pitcher and hitter, operated out of Stromsburg but pitched for many other teams in both the PNL and the NIL and for non-league teams as well, such as Sandy's strong 1946 and 1947 Goetz team in Lincoln. If pressed for a hometown base and loyalty, though, Max would probably have named Stromsburg.

During that same year Bob Cerv appeared with both Wahoo and Pender and at least once for David City in the PNL, as well as briefly for Lexington in the NIL playoffs before signing with the New York Yankees. Bill Denker, later a regular with Lexington and a one-year mainstay with North Platte (both in the NIL), also saw action with both Pender and Wahoo. Harlan "Buzz" Powley, a regular with Pender in 1948, later played for North Platte. (Cerv, Denker, and Powley, plus Del Blatchford, Bill Jensen, Bob Bull, Angelo Ossino, and Bob Diers—all of whom played in the PNL and more than half of whom played in the NIL—were all teammates of mine at the University of Nebraska.) Despite some league switching, however, the majority of the PNL players remained fixed with their teams, unlike many in the constantly evolving and overhauled NIL teams during the 1948–55 period.

During the six years I played in the NIL there was always a quiet rivalry with the PNL. We each thought we were the better league, and it was truly unfortunate that the fans never got to find out which one actually was through a regular interleague playoff series. It is certain that the gates would have been very large, just from curiosity alone. But both leagues were already straining to hold teams intact for their own established end-of-season playoffs, which occurred at the time of the year when teams were breaking up and losing player personnel to fall commitments.

I myself played, just once, for a PNL team, and it turned out to be an experience that taught me—the hard way—the lesson of keeping your head in the game. Just after the 1949 NU season ended and before I moved back to McCook for a second summer in the refurbished and still very exciting NIL, Coach Tony Sharpe asked me if I wanted to take a ride to David City and play second base in one game while he played third, a position he had once handled very well in the minor leagues. A few extra bucks sounded good for travel money to McCook, so I said yes.

Shortly before the game I found out the team we would be playing against had a barnstormer—the infamous and unfortunate Mickey Owen of Brooklyn Dodgers notoriety, whose failure to catch a careening curve ball (or was it a "spit ball"?) on a swinging third strike led to eventual disaster for the Dodgers in the 1941 World Series. Mickey had had troubles after that as well: he went to Mexico to play some baseball, apparently without getting the baseball commissioner's permission, and was suspended. During that suspension he was barnstorming around the country, picking up some money on the notoriety of his unfortunate World Series mistake.

I watched Mickey during infield practice. He was smooth and he had a good arm but was no better than Bill Kinnamon (of Sandy's Goetz), P. O. Karthauser (of McCook), or Tommy O'Connor (later with North Platte). The game started, and before long Owen was on second. I was only a few yards away from him, so I studied this suspended major leaguer to see if I could find any unique quality that separated him from us. I couldn't; he was just an average guy in a baseball uniform. But my attention was on *him* more than on holding a runner close to second.

My research study was interrupted suddenly when Bob Cerv hit the tallest pop fly in the history of baseball. As the ball sped upward and completely disappeared high above the lights, I estimated it would be coming down somewhere in the territory I was supposed to cover, unfortunately behind me. I drifted back and searched for any sign of the ball. There was none, but I knew there had to be soon. The hang time on that fly ball seemed like five minutes, though of course it was less. Finally I spotted it in reentry and staggered about trying to get under it in short right field. The right fielder had not called me off. He didn't want it. He probably couldn't even find it. Then it was hurtling toward my left shoulder with a speed I was sure would tear the glove off my hand. I lurched to the left and made the catch. In numb relief, I lobbed the ball toward the infield and began trotting to the dugout.

After only a few steps I was aware that something was amiss.

Mickey Owen, who had tagged up at second, immediately sprinted to third, where Tony Sharpe stood dumbfounded as the second baseman he had recommended, who obviously thought there'd been two outs before the catch and had lobbed the ball to nobody in particular, headed off the field. I stopped in shock at this realization and averted my eyes from an infield full of angry and disbelieving stares. I didn't even want to think of what Tony and Mickey were saying to each other over at third base. I looked for a hole to crawl into.

What happened after that to end the inning is just a blank. My mind was totally occupied searching for a plan to stay away from our dugout. I wondered if I could just hang around with the other second baseman when he came out. I would promise not to get in the way. Just give me one inning while they cooled down. Tony had always said he could accept physical errors, but he didn't care one bit for mental errors. Fortunately, my dumb play didn't cost us the game, so driving back to Lincoln wasn't as bad as it could have been. I think I even caught Tony chuckling once.

Several years later I ran across an article that lifted a great weight off my shoulders. It was wonderful to have distinguished company from the absolute top of the field: Joe DiMaggio had actually had such a mental lapse. In a game that was tied 2–2, Gerry Priddy and George Kell had doubled and put the Detroit Tigers in front. Steve Souchock flied deep to DiMaggio. Kell tagged up and raced for third. But Joe, instead of throwing the ball quickly to the cutoff man, started trotting toward the Yankee dugout, head down to check the ball before tossing it to the umpire or the mound. The Tiger third base coach recognized the mistake before Joe did and immediately waved Kell on around to score. Dimaggio, red-faced, later said he'd thought it was the third out.

Yeah. Joe D. and me. We had our own private club.

In reassessing Mickey Owen, I decided one of the differences between him and me was his trained ability to keep his head in the game, any game, at all times. Even out in the farmlands of Nebraska. Mickey was tagged up and leaning toward third when I caught that ball, even though it wasn't deep enough for him to advance to third. But when I flipped it to no one, he was off like a shot. He may have missed Hugh Casey's pitch. Physical error. But mental discipline kept him from lagging off second, so that he wouldn't have to race back and tag up before going to third.

I read somewhere that Dimaggio once listed among his strongest memories a game in which he dropped two fly balls. And of all the hundreds of fine catches Joe made, I'm sure jogging to the dugout with the ball in his hand when there were only two outs is another of his clearest and least favorite recollections.

The Cornhusker League towns clustered east and west in a close grouping in the southeastern section of the state. Four of them— Aurora, York, Utica, and Seward—were located in an almost straight line west to east between Grand Island and Lincoln, just north of present Interstate 80. Osceola is only about twenty-five miles north of York, Geneva and Sutton about the same distance south, and Central City less than twenty miles north of Aurora, near the Platte River. This eight-team semi-pro league operated with much greater convenience in regard to team travel than either the NIL or the PNL.

Undoubtedly the most celebrated player connected with the Cornhusker League was the Nebraska-born major league star Clarence Mitchell, who is in fact credited with having done much to create that league. This hard-hitting left-hander had an eighteen-year career as a good hitting pitcher and a fine outfielder. Mitchell developed one of the best spitballs of all time and was one of the pitchers who qualified to continue using it after the pitch was banned by Commissioner Kennesaw Mountain Landis. Clarence was the only left-hander using the spitball through the 1920s and up to his retirement in 1932. After retiring from the major leagues, Mitchell settled in Aurora, Nebraska, and became a playing manager for the town's Cornhusker League entry. He continued managing the Aurora team until the regular league membership was disbanded in 1953.

In 1955 the state of Nebraska saw a general disbanding and reorganization of a dying form of the national pastime. The once thriving two-division Pioneer Nite League had wilted to a four-team shadow of its formerly vigorous self; by 1955 only Columbus, Wahoo, Schuyler, and David City continued to compete under the PNL heading.

In 1956 the Cornhusker League climbed back on its feet and resumed activity with a new assemblage of teams. The New Cornhusker League combined former PNL and Cornhusker towns plus a couple of others: York, Utica, Genoa, Wahoo, Stromsburg, Sutton, Columbus, Schuyler, and Crete played out the year.

Who Are Those Guys
Anyway?

Returning in late May 1949 to our basement apartment in McCook, Don and I were welcomed by hard-working, shy Mrs. Pearl Fagan and her forty-year-old daughter Beryl. Pearl was very self-conscious about a large goiter swelling on the right side of her neck. It was the first thing I had noticed when I met her, and I always thought it must have interfered substantially with her housework and cooking, but I never once heard her complain about it.

I still had my sportswriting job at the *Gazette*. I was happy that my 1948 efforts had been satisfactory, at least to local readers (except once when I didn't compute the batting averages accurately). I may have offended some readers from the other NIL towns, though, with my casual and, I thought, humorous treatment of league incidents. I would wonder about that later when I became aware of certain attitudes toward me among other league players. If I had it to do over, I would hesitate about taking such a job while also playing ball. But at the time, I remember, other job options were not very interesting or plentiful.

When we all got together again at Eastside Ballpark, I was pleased to see that the nucleus of our very successful team of the year before was basically the same. There would be a few pitching changes: Bill Gardner was back and on the staff full time; Eddie McCarthy would start and pitch part of the season for the Cats; and managing and pitching in 1949 would be Dave Garland, an enormously talented pitcher who'd been signed by the St. Louis Browns in 1940 as a "bonus baby" but who dropped out later to finish medi-

Kermit Lewis

cal school. Dave had spent the 1948 season pitching in Denver and very briefly in McCook.

Replacing local right fielder Babe Fidler was Bobby West from Denver, a battling little left-hander with a very accurate throwing arm and an incurable habit of getting on base. One time, at bat at Holdrege against Ralph Germano, also from Denver, Bobby was determined to demonstrate why he was considered a very tough out. With two strikes, he methodically fouled off eight or nine tough pitches. Germano slammed the ball into his glove, hitched up his pants, and fired another fast ball to West. Again the gritty little right fielder fouled the pitch back over the grandstand.

Germano leaned forward, muttering curses to himself, and took the sign. He broke his slow curve ball off, and once more Bobby nicked it into the dirt. After several more fouls Ralph turned around and began talking violently to his shoes, the infield, the base coach, saying, "I'll be a this and that!" He again took his sign and came off the mound with everything he had. West spit some tobacco juice aside contemptuously and mechanically fouled it off the screen.

At this, Ralph lost his head. He reached down, grabbed up the rosin bag, and fired it toward the plate. Though surprised, Bobby waited as the little white bag flopped its way to him and then swung. Missing intentionally, he sent the entire grandstand into laughter and broke the unbearable tension in that very important game.

Dave Garland was to many hitters the most bewildering and annoying right-hander in the league. He stood about six-foot-two; with his long, limber arms he had the "looseness" on the mound of a Satchel Paige or Diz Dean and commanded a wide assortment of pitches with different speeds. His sidearm fast ball absolutely froze hitters after they had seen a tightly spinning, slow curve ball creeping up and off the outside corner from a low sidearm delivery. This pitch defied gravity; traveling that slowly it should have lost altitude, but it didn't. It even seemed to rise higher as it buzzed off the corner. He would then change pace with a crackling overhand fast curve or a high fast ball.

I still have in my memory a very clear image of Garland's pitching motions, the different arm heights of release, the different speeds and movement on the pitches. I spent a lot of time looking over his left shoulder and marveling at the variety of stuff the ball had when he dispatched it plateward. Garland was a bit of a showman and at times had some fun on the mound with his juggling ability. Some considered him cocky and a big hotdog. I have seen him look to the catcher to get the sign while rotating the baseball over and over with just the first two fingers and thumb of his pitching hand. Then he would drop it and straighten out his arm casually. The ball would bounce off the biceps of his pitching arm, land softly on the back of the two extended fingers, roll down his straightened arm and across his shoulders, and drop into his glove, which suddenly was behind his back. Finally, without a pause, he would smoothly deliver a blazing fast ball over the inside corner, causing the mesmerized batter, still staring at Garland, to call time out while he figured out what had just happened.

The whole procedure was so fascinating that I was determined to learn how to do it to impress my friends—like a magic trick. I practiced for hours until I became exhausted from picking up the drops and spinoffs. I never felt ready for prime time, but I did gain serious appreciation of the absolute need for long, flexible fingers as well as good juggling instincts.

Other clubs in the NIL had been temporarily stunned and angry when the cellar-dwelling Cats leaped to first by hiring outside talent. But it was only a matter of time before parity was established, as other clubs followed McCook's serious and expensive program of improvement.

Holdrege fans looked out on the diamond in 1949 and said, "Wait a minute. Who are those guys? Tom Sutak, Bobby Lott, Jack Baxter, Rich Hotton, Len Hawkins? Where are Herschel Rinehart, Al Beinhoff, Dale Meisenbach, or Marks and Hansen and Landin?" They reached for their nonexistent programs to see if they were at the right game.

Rich Hotton had played third base for the Denver Bears in the Class A Western League the year before; Tom Sutak and Len

Hawkins were outstanding and expensive semi-pros from Denver; and Bobby Lott and Jack Baxter were smooth-fielding stars from Denver University. A lot of hometown players were suddenly riding the bench or even out of uniform in Holdrege.

Little Superior, having no idea what lay ahead in financial commitment, was serious in its desire to play with the NIL fast laners, who found two additional teams in 1949: newcomer Grand Island, and Hastings, making another try. Unlike the on-and-off Hastings entry, however, the Knights came to play and stay, as the *Superior Weekly Journal* assured local fans: "No effort has been spared by manager [Kermit] Lewis and the Chamber of Commerce committee in their attempt to field a winning team. By the second or third game, a better balanced squad should be ready."

Joe Paniak, a Class B hurler from Joplin, Missouri, was brought in to pitch the 1949 opener for Superior; McCook batted around in the first inning to welcome Joe to the NIL. Leo Romano from Chicago, observed Superior sportswriter Jerry Pickerell, "found the pace too fast both in the field and at bat." Bill Harmsen, former International League pitcher, did better, lasting nine full innings. With management searching for the magic touch, Hal Bart was flown in from the West Coast to play shortstop. Still, Superior faced hard times throughout the 1949 season.

The "Here's Sports" column of the June 14, 1949, *Holdrege Citizen* reported that the radical change in makeup of the Holdrege Bears had caught the suspicious eye of North Platte sports columnists, who sensed a dangerous and rapid trend emerging in the NIL. To Jimmy Kirkman, a North Platte writer who had "tagged the Holdrege Bears an imported team with each member working in Holdrege and playing baseball just for the fun of it," the Holdrege paper responded, "Have it your way, Jimmy. As long as we win, we're satisfied."

But what Kirkman was really saying, and other people were also noticing, was that McCook's new lineup and stunning results had started a rush in the NIL to round up from near and far all the talent money could buy, and fast. Holdrege's success was illustrated by the immediate and dazzling change in double-play numbers. Denver imports Sutak, Lott, Hotton, and Baxter had turned thirty-three twin killings by August 6, 1949—eleven better than second-place Kearney—and this on a league schedule averaging fewer than three games a week.

So successful in establishing parity was the far-reaching recruiting for the entire league that from 1948 to 1953 five different towns won the NIL's regular season title. In 1953 the race was so tight that even the fifth place team—Superior, with 15 wins and 15 losses—was at .500 and the winner only at .613. Kearney took first place with a 19-and-12 record after playing off an 18-and-12 tie with McCook, and Lexington and North Platte were forced to play off a 16-and-14 tie for third and fourth.

In just one startling year, McCook had set the league on an irreversible and escalating course of player spending, which alarmed those guarding the coffers and sent veteran sportswriters into the streets waving their arms about danger to the towns' dwindling wealth as well as the future of NIL baseball.

But the NIL townspeople didn't want to hear this. The ballplayers were riding high, attendance was way up, and excitement about the league had never been greater. We'll worry about it tomorrow, we all decided. If certain towns (like Hastings) couldn't afford to stay in anymore, let them drop out and quit criticizing the league. After all, the quality of baseball had never been so good.

The Grand Island Incident

I was not regarded as a long ball hitter, so when I timed Art Dollaghan's first-pitch fast ball just right and drove it over the left-field fence my first time up, it turned everyone's head on our bench. And because it gave us our second run in a very important game against Grand Island near the end of the 1949 season in a tight league race, I was greeted with great excitement and smiles of happy amazement when I rounded home.

Big Art Dollaghan, NIL strikeout king of 1949, angrily proceeded to mow down nearly everyone else in our lineup with his blazing fast ball, and then I was up again. I was feeling especially proud because the heavy hitters were having trouble getting to Dollaghan, and I was loose because I had my 1 for 3 already. Anything else off hard-throwing Art would be a bonus.

Dollaghan, convinced my home run was a complete mistake, kicked and blazed his number-one express down the middle again where he'd been striking out everybody all year. I was right on it again. The ball traveled over the left-field fence at almost the identical location of the first one, and we had two more runs. I circled the bases quickly and came to the bench unable to hold back a smile.

"I don't know what's the matter," I said, trying not to let Dollaghan see my delight. My teammates' faces betrayed stunned disbelief, almost resentment, even though they were smiling.

The score was still 4 to 0 when I came to bat for the third time. Our big hitters had been practically handcuffed to this point, so I thought this night it was up to me, and I prepared to jump on his fast

Art Dollaghan

ball one more time while I was hot. It was one of those nights when you can see the ball really well, and though Art's fast ball had others popping up, I had it timed. I was ready again.

Dollaghan delivered. I picked up the ball right off his fingertips, but it wasn't down the middle this time. It was right on the bill of my cap, and very big. I went on my back. The bat flew up. My cap went another direction, and I was certain the ball had made contact with it. I had heard the expression "turn his cap around," but never before was I part of the demonstration. I got to my feet and dusted myself off, my knees feeling a bit wobbly. That was close, I thought. It was the first time I had been knocked down by a ninety-mile-an-hour fast ball. I dug in, determined to drive one back at his kneecaps to get even. Same pitch. I went down again. Dusting myself off again, I looked at Umpire McCoy in anger, as if I expected him to do something about it. But in 1949, in frontier semi-pro baseball, there was no such thing as warning the pitcher. And there were no batting helmets.

I dug in again. I went down again. I took my time getting myself together. I must have really got to Art, I thought. He was a madman. He must have seen me smiling on the bench after all. I did a little math and concluded that now he would have to throw a strike (or walk me, which I was certain would be as unsatisfactory to Art as my getting another hit). I knew it would be a fast ball and I was ready. Dollaghan blazed three angry fast balls. I took three furious swings but didn't get more than a loud foul.

I went to my second base position brooding about the next time at bat. I would get him this time. Should I drag a bunt to the first baseman to make Art cover first and then run him over when he covered, as Enos Slaughter of the St. Louis Cardinals was known to do? No, I wanted to scald one back through the middle and turn *his* cap around. For eight batters I fumed. Then I was up for the fourth time. By then I didn't even know what the score was. I dug in. I was going to line one off his kneecaps.

I went down again. If possible, this pitch was even closer than the others; I was certain it had hit my cap. Later I kicked myself for not jumping up and grabbing my cap, pointing to it furiously, and trotting down to first. I am sure McCoy would have allowed it. Instead, I got up, glared at Dollaghan, turned to McCoy (who was looking at his indicator), and cleaned myself up. By now the assault had jarred me into the middle of the real NIL world. I no longer felt like the reporter taking notes at an accident; I felt like the victim. In those days I never saw anybody charge the mound when dusted. It just wasn't done. Knockdown pitches were part of the game, and if you didn't like it, you hit another home run or a line drive at the pitcher's head. Or if you played for the right team, your pitcher would take care of one of them to get even.

I looked over to Bill Gardner, our pitcher, then to P. O. Karthauser, and then to Dollaghan, my glare signaling "you know what to do when *he* comes up." I dug in again. I went down again. This time I walked over near our dugout as I dusted myself off and looked at Gardner as if to say, "You want me to keep picking up your grounders (and I was having a great defensive night too), you had better knock this sonofabitch down!"

I went down again. Ball three. I had had it. I almost went out after Dollaghan, but reconsidered. I would have been thrown out of the game. Besides that, Art was six-foot-three and 210 pounds, and I was five-foot-eleven and 160. No, he had to come in now with some strikes, and I would get him this time. Three blazing fast balls. I had three really good hacks but missed. I probably overstrode and swung under them, because the timing was there. It never occurred to me to take a pitch or two. McCoy might have called one a ball out of sympathy.

When I sat down on our bench, drained, no one said a word to me. I felt hurt, confused, and angry. So far, Dollaghan had not even been brushed back, and I had gone down six times, undoubtedly a league record—possibly a world record. I was completely demoralized. The elation of my two home runs and three runs batted in had been completely wiped out. I had never felt such a sense of dejected confusion and betrayal. I was winning a very important game down the stretch almost single-handedly and nearly getting killed while my teammates were looking the other way and whistling, and my pitcher was plugging away as if none of this were happening. With

Bill Gardner pitching for us that night—a guy who had such good stuff he didn't even have to pitch inside, and who was nicer than Robin Roberts—my chances for brushback protection were worse than slim and none.

As the game went on, I became more bewildered by his and the rest of my team's acceptance of my being mugged from the mound. If I had to *ask* Gardner to provide payback and protection for me, there was something very wrong with this whole arrangement. Did they blame me for Dollaghan's being almost unhittable that night? He didn't even move any of them off the plate, since they hadn't done any damage to him, and it appeared that my teammates wanted to keep it that way. Was it simply a matter of "better him than me" when Art got that mad? It was one of the first times I experienced a lack of "team" in baseball. I seemed to be on my own, no matter what I did for the team.

As I thought about this game over the years, I almost lost sight of the fact that we won 4 to 0 and that I drove in three of our four runs and had a great night defensively too. One of my greatest games had turned into one of my most disturbing sports experiences, to be relived many times. The disappointment in my own teammates, especially in our pitcher and catcher for letting me twist in the wind, was greater than my anger at Dollaghan. After all, I had embarrassed him, and I did beat him in a very important game.

Among my fantasies reflecting on "Artful" revenge, the most satisfying scenario has the Grand Baseball-Bum Genie visiting me from out of his bottle in the late innings of that game and whispering that for five minutes I could have the loan and mastery of one Smokey Molden fast ball, one Max Quick fast ball, one Tommy Hurd fast ball, and one Fred Wells curve ball (Hurd and Wells to be documented later). When Dollaghan comes to bat for the last time, I calmly walk over to Bill Gardner on the mound and say, "Bill, sit this one out. Go play second base while I pitch to this guy."

My first pitch is the Fred Wells terrible big-breaking roaring curve ball, which appears to start for Art's head at a frightening speed and produces such jelly legs in the batter's box that Art loses his balance and falls on his ass as the ball veers down across the high-inside corner of the plate and Umpire McCoy shouts, "Strike."

The next selection is the Max Quick express up and under the chin, which turns Dollaghan two shades whiter than white and puts him flat on his back. Next, I send the Tommy Hurd knee-high lightning bolt, which Dollaghan angrily says sounded low and asks McCoy to see the ball to prove I actually threw one. McCoy tells Karthauser to show him the ball and says, "That would be strike two, Mr. Dollaghan."

The Smokey Molden heavy rocket bat-and-hand destroyer is my final offering to angry Art. It comes around from behind the back on a near-sidearm delivery, appears briefly to be over the middle of the plate, but then stealthily relocates itself on the inside corner, feeling like a fifteen-ounce rock, shattering Art's bat below the trademark, and leaving his vibrating hands numb for more than three innings. The ball dribbles pathetically back to the mound and I lob it to first as the pained and humiliated opposing pitcher staggers toward first, unable to let go of the shattered and vibrating bat handle.

Now, that fantasy should have put the "Grand Island Incident" to rest and restored peace in my tormented NIL memory bank. It should have, but it didn't.

In the later 1940s and early 1950s, long before the accepted and required use of batting helmets, we did as in Rome. There was a code to play by, and if you were going to step in with the big boys, you played by it or went home. This code sometimes defied common sense with regard to safety. Football players finally became smart enough to wear helmets, but it took baseball players many more years to admit that ducking a ninety-mile-an-hour fast ball with only a cloth cap on the head was about the dumbest thing to put up with in an otherwise exciting but reasonably non-life-threatening, intelligently conceived game. The unprotected-head policy existed in the same thoughtful tradition as spitting tobacco juice on a spike wound.

Buck Leonard, a great Negro league first baseman of the 1930s and 1940s, has reminded everyone of what it was like in those days.

"They would throw at your head, legs, anytime. And we didn't have helmets then. Pitchers were not fined or thrown out of the game for throwing at your head. You had to learn how to duck as well as hit. That was just one more thing on your mind."

I had heard back when I was about twelve that the parents of the boys playing in the Omaha younger leagues watched in great anxiety as big Rex Barney (later to pitch for the Brooklyn Dodgers) fired incredibly swift and also wild fast balls toward their sons, who had nothing but a cloth cap with a cardboard bill to protect their heads. And later, when I coached my own sons in Little League baseball on Long Island, I was thankful that hard plastic helmets with double ear flaps and thick foam rubber padding were required protection, especially as I watched pitchers who stood a head taller than the other ten- to twelve-year-olds, and who peaked at age fourteen, throw bullets from a distance of forty-five feet.

My dad realized when we were young that some of the bigger kids who could throw much harder than the others posed a serious danger to less-experienced, slower-to-react batters. He searched for and finally located an old leather head protector, modified it, and urged us to wear it under or over our caps when we batted. But because nobody wore protective headgear then, we were not going to be teased about it, so we refused.

Two years after the Grand Island Incident, while playing for North Platte in the NIL, I really was beaned. I spent the night in and out of consciousness with my head on an icebag in the hospital. Our third baseman, Ronnie Bennett, said that after I went down, my legs were twitching. I never asked him if he was kidding or not. Ironically, that ball was thrown by a friend, Chuck Wright, a hard-hurling right-hander who had pitched for us at the University of Nebraska. Chuck wasn't even trying to move me back from the plate. He just let his hard curve ball get away too soon, and it came in high and behind me, boring down. I spun my head around instinctively and was in the process of ducking when over Chuck's and the catcher's shouts of "Look out!" I felt and heard the ball make absolutely solid contact with the base of my skull. They carried me off on a stretcher, semiconscious.

I was back playing within a few days, and it wasn't until I read what Jimmy Kirkman wrote for his column in the *North Platte Telegraph-Bulletin* a day or so after the ball knocked me out that I realized the seriousness of what we were doing every time we went up to bat: "We doubt if Hobe Hays, North Platte's popular second sacker, is available for duty this Sunday night. . . . The pitched ball struck him just above the neck on the back of his head, a vital nerve spot. The blow could have killed him, so he is still lucky."

I thought of Ray Chapman and Carl Mays. In 1920 Cleveland Indians' Chapman had been killed right in the batter's box of Yankee Stadium by Mays's terrifying submarine pitch, which struck Ray in the head. I was knocked out by a curve ball traveling about seventy-five miles an hour. Dollaghan had thrown six fast balls with pin-point control at close to ninety miles an hour, aiming intentionally at my head. The more I thought about it in later years, the more I wondered why it took so long to institute the warning-the-pitcher rule, and only then after batting helmets had become required equipment. It was a wonder that Chapman had been the only fatality at the plate in the big leagues.

I also tried to remember why I let the thing at Grand Island go to six knockdown pitches without throwing my bat at Dollaghan's shins on a hard swinging strike. I remember how surprised I was each time he followed with another. Each one, I kept thinking, was the last, so I kept digging in with angry spikes to hit another one out. But contrary to Tony Sharpe's theory, getting me mad did not help the timing of my swing; it only made the swing angrier.

After the shock of nearly having my head knocked off six times (I was very impressed with Art's control—he would have scored on each of those pitches if I had not removed my head just in time), I tried to figure out why this unforgettable incident ever took place. I had always thought of myself as a guy fairly easy to get along with and not looking for trouble, a quiet player innocently going about my business on the ball field. How could two sudden home runs, which surprised me as much as Dollaghan, turn baseball from action fun to something so threatening to my health?

Later, research and review began to give me some possible answers. In reading old sports pages I came across this statement from Walt Charlesworth's column in the August 18, 1948, *Holdrege Citizen*, written the year he caught for Holdrege: "Hobe Hays, who hit well for U.N. has finally hit his stride—with the Cats. Hobe has knocked out 9 hits in the last 3 ball games. Hobe was the hero of the Cats pennant winner against Kearney, and who knows but that Hobe may be another Tommy Thevenow and lead the Cats to a play-off win as well. Hobe will be a marked man from here on out." That may have been said tongue-in-cheek, but in 1949 Charlesworth was catching that Grand Island game, and it's possible he remembered his words from the year before.

Another thing I noticed was that of all ten of my home runs in the NIL, I had hit four of them off Dollaghan by 1949. Art, knowing I was no cleanup hitter and being the strikeout king of the league, may have bristled at my output at his expense. Putting it all together, I actually did seem to have become a marked man.

There were words I would like to have said during those moments of anger and confusion in the Grand Island Incident, words that have since passed through my mind in many forms. I would like to have turned to Walt and said, "Are you calling those knockdown pitches, Walt? I know big Art is a little hot because I've hit two of his best fast balls over the left-field wall. He is young and his pride is hurt because he's the league's strikeout champion, and there's a lot riding on this game."

"Yeah, I'm calling them," Charlesworth might have snarled. "This isn't 'college hotdog' baseball anymore, Hays. If you don't like it, you can always quit and go home."

"Walt," I might have replied, "you are a wise old veteran, and even if Art is too mad to realize it, you know he can throw hard enough to kill a person if the ball hits the guy's head. Have you forgotten this is just a game?"

"No, this isn't just a game, Hays," Walt might have snapped. "This is bread and butter. Winning and losing is pretty damned important to most of us here. If teams can't make it to the playoffs, they may not have the money to pay the players. Just look at Hastings."

And then I would have realized, as I do now, that NIL baseball was not "just a game," as it had been for me, but a contest of survival in a group of small towns where an original idea of baseball for fun had gotten far out of control; unfortunately, it had become a serious and at times very dangerous business.

Nobody Had Seen
That Kind of Power
Around Here

Toward the end of August in the 1949 NIL season, I was surprised one night to see two new players in uniform in our dugout. I thought our team was pretty well set in personnel, but I shouldn't have been caught off balance, because new faces were always appearing at Shaughnessy playoff times.

One of the new men was an outfielder about six-foot-four with broad shoulders, long arms, and huge hands. His name was Horace Garner. The other was Mickey Stubblefield, a muscular five-foot-nine athlete who pitched and could play all the other positions as well—especially second base. When I learned this last fact, I rechecked my batting average from the year before. I remembered hitting .324 for the regular season, so I thought they must have Mickey here for other reasons, like pitching. But why another outfielder, when we had McElreath, Miller, and West? Only then did I notice that Al McElreath was no longer in our midst. I would not learn why until years later.

Horace and Mickey were both black. At that time, though the Chicago Cubs' great shortstop Ernie Banks was reported to have played briefly at Superior a few years before, and Lacey Curry had played some third base at McCook, the NIL was all white. Except for Smokey Molden and one or two other people I had known in Lincoln, the capital city was nearly all white. Until Horace and Mickey arrived, I could not remember seeing any blacks in McCook.

Both men had come from the Kansas City Stars' exhibition team (Garner had also played with Jacksonville in the old Southern As-

Horace Garner

sociation). When teams such as the Stars and the Kansas City Monarchs came to play in NIL towns in the 1940s and 1950s, they were usually referred to in print as "colored"; there was never any thought that this word might be offensive. With the same lack of sensitivity, a player who was black would always be identified as "colored pitcher Smokey Molden" or "colored outfielder Horace Garner."

Despite the extremely high percentage of white players in the NIL, though, as long as I played with and against Horace and Mickey, I never heard any racial insults from players or fans, at home or away. First of all, you would be a fool to insult Horace because, though it took a lot to erase the friendly smile on his face, if it did get erased, he might just take you apart. If you decided to run, I would put my money on Horace to run you down, even if you were state sprint champion. And happy Mickey would be nobody to insult either, with his 98 percent muscle-tone frame. But during my experience in the NIL I never saw or heard any sign of anyone starting trouble with racial insults, and I never heard other players speak of any such incidents.

Garner was spectacular on a baseball field. With his outstanding speed he looked like a combination of the New York Yankees' Dave Winfield and Bernie Williams when he ran the bases. And Horace's strong right arm stopped the others in their tracks when he threw to third and home at the end of infield practice. Folks seeing him throw for the first time just turned to one another with slack jaws and large eyes. One night Horace stunned the fans with a little demonstration before the game: he stood by home plate on the foul side of the first base line and threw the ball all the way in the air to the 400-foot marker on the center-field fence.

As for hitting, some of Garner's blows had to be seen to be believed. In one game at Holdrege I was in the on-deck circle on the first base side (I was having an unusual hot streak of power hitting and was batting in the unfamiliar fifth slot), so I had a great view of that particular at-bat. The pitch was a knee-high fast ball on the outside part of the plate, and "Hoss," who had just had a couple of bad strikes called on him and was a little hot, smashed it to dead center on the trajectory of a Sam Snead one-iron shot. The pitcher didn't just flinch; he ducked and fell down. The ball was out of the park so fast I think it was still going up when it cleared the center-field fence. I had seen Bob Cerv hit some long home runs at Nebraska U., but this one was the quickest to leave a park I had ever seen, and I'll never forget the echoing wood sound as he crushed that ball. And Horace sent many more like that one whistling fenceward. Some stayed in the park only because they were hit too low to the ground and with too much top spin, causing them to dive down into the fence.

By August 10, 1950, Horace's first full year in the NIL, he was hitting just eight points under .400, with 22 runs batted in, 23 runs scored, 5 home runs, and 13 stolen bases in just 84 at-bats. Garner had everything needed to play in the major leagues. He was just born fifteen years too soon. "He never could quite make it to the majors," Ed Miller said later in a *McCook Gazette* interview. "I think his age was against him. He was just too old when they broke that color barrier."

When Don Lindstrom of the *Holdrege Citizen* called Horace a poor fielder because he "couldn't go back on a fly ball," I felt it necessary to enlighten Donnie. The truth was that Garner could catch anything that stayed in the park and go back on a fly ball as well as any outfielder. It was just that he had no fondness for snakes, and he refused to plunge blindly into the dark and forbidding foliage of some of the league's outfields after finding that dead snake by the right-field fence in Fairgrounds Park and hearing reports of another one found in right-center at Kearney. The fact that they were both real dead didn't matter.

Manhattan, Kansas, was a small college town of about fourteen thousand. It was the home of Kansas State University, member of the Big Seven Conference, and we Nebraska Cornhuskers had come to play a two-day doubleheader with the Wildcats.

After supper following the Friday game, with time on our hands, some of us went out for a look around the campus. We put on our reversible letter jackets with the big white "N" on a red wool body with gray suede leather sleeves and ventured into the cool Kansas night air to impress the K-State coeds.

We didn't really have any big plans in mind, and Coach Tony Sharpe had told us to be in early so we would be in shape for the Saturday afternoon game. There usually wasn't anything big going on in Manhattan, Kansas, anyway except the basketball games; during this period they were as big as the games in neighboring Lawrence, where the national powerhouse Kansas Jayhawks nested. In the early 1950s Kansas State was definitely a match for the University of Kansas, and the intrastate rivalry not only was fierce and personal but very noteworthy, since few states could boast two such nationally ranked teams.

As we sauntered along "checking out the chicks," we all were vaguely trying to think of something to do. "I saw a poster that said there was a dance here on campus tonight," outfielder/pitcher Jim Sharp said. "Let's be goers." The rest of us—Harlan "Buzz" Powley, quiet and strong outfielder with surprising power at bat; Bill Jensen, excellent utility infielder who had the arm to play any position; Bob Lohrberg, fine all-round catcher; Bob Diers, heavy-hitting outfielder; Bob Camp, hard-throwing right handed pitcher; and I—went into a quick conference and returned a verdict: "Let's at least check it out."

At the entrance to the dance hall we inquired about the price of tickets and were told that it was three dollars apiece. That plus the curfew-imposed shortness of the evening somewhat dampened our enthusiasm for entering.

"Ahoya!" Jim Sharp said. "I've got a plan! This is a great idea. Each of you give me a dollar, and I'll pay to go into the dance, and—"

"That's six dollars," Bill Jensen said. "You're making four bucks' profit right at the start."

"That does sound like a great idea, Jim," Buzz Powley said. "You go in and dance, and we'll wait outside for you."

"What are you doing here, Buzz?" Jim said. "Don't you have a date tonight? You make out on every other road trip we take."

"The quietest guy on the team, and he always has a date," I said.

"Yeah, Powley," Bob Lohrberg said, "we don't usually see you until game time."

"Wait a minute, wait a minute," Bob Diers said. "We're getting sidetracked. Is there more to your plan, or is it as stupid as it sounds?"

"Let's be listeners, now," Jim said. "As I was saying, I will go in, paying with three of your dollars. After a few minutes I'll tell the ticket-taker that I have to get something from my car, and he will stamp the back of my hand so that I can get back in."

"Oh, that's different," Bob Camp said. "That's worth a dollar to me."

"Once I'm back outside," Jim continued, "the beauty part of the plan begins. Hobe, you will then copy the stamp from the back of my hand on all you guys' hands, and you all walk into the dance free."

"Me?" I said. "Copy it! With what? That would take all night."

"You're the artist," Jim said. "It will be easy for you."

"We'll never fool the stamp guy at the door," I said.

"Let's be doers!" Sharp said, holding out his hand for contributions. "Four bucks between all of you. The price has come down."

"It costs *three* bucks to get in!" Jensen said.

"That's what I said," Jim said. "Three bucks among all of us. Fifty cents apiece."

The money was donated, and Jim Sharp—having donated only the plan—walked into the building with his quick step while we all wandered around looking at the cars and stars, waiting for our strong-armed outfielder/pitcher/idea-man to return.

Soon he did, and I looked at the stamp on the back of his hand under the streetlight, fearing a detailed and complicated design with letters. To my relief, the stamp was an indistinct circular design, which I felt I could successfully fake.

"Who's got a pen?" I said. "With black ink." Fortunately, the stamp was from a black ink pad, not a red one; we might have been in trouble trying to find a pen with red ink. I began slowly and carefully on the first one, sketching lightly the general composition of the stamp, then delicately filling in areas to simulate the total impression.

"Ahoya!" Jim said. "Let's be listeners again! Don't go in there together, and don't go right away. It's too early, and the stamp guy will remember who has left. Wait until a few more people have come and gone." We all nodded in agreement. This was a very important point of strategy that we had almost overlooked. The whole caper could have blown up in our faces if we had all rushed in too soon together.

Some of us turned our reversible jackets inside out so that we wouldn't be quite so obvious. Then, one by one, spacing our individual entrances with care as a number of K-State students exited and entered the dance, we sauntered casually up to the ticket-taker, exposed our "stamped" hands, and calmly strolled in to size up the girl situation.

I don't remember how many hits I got that series, but I do know I *was* the hit of that road trip, as the tale of the K-State dance-stamp heist was told and retold many times on the trip back to Lincoln.

The 1950 Nebraska season was marked by highs and lows for me. I sprained my ankle a couple of times and missed a few games, and then late in the season I remember a sharp pain shooting through the outside of my left foot as I came down hard on it, lunging for a hot ground ball to my left. I tried to shake it off, but it bothered me the rest of the game, and I was aware of some pain with every step as I went to my classes the next few days. When we played again, I asked to have it taped. The pain was constant but bearable. I didn't say anything to Tony Sharpe at first and tried to hide my limp, but somebody noticed my unnatural gait, and my picture appeared on the May 4, 1950, *Lincoln Star* sports page with the caption, "Hobe Hays has been slowed by an ankle injury and may not see action Friday and Saturday when the Cornhuskers entertain Kansas in a two-game Big Seven series." I played hurt and got 4 for 7 in the two games.

The foot continued to bother me. The May 19, 1950, *Star* published the same picture, saying, "Hobe Hays is a question mark as the Huskers entertain Colorado's baseball team at the N.U. diamond Friday and Saturday afternoons. A leg injury may shelve Hays from his regular second base post." I tried to play the series, but after getting a hit through the middle my first time up I had to come out of the game. I could not run, no matter how much I thought of Tom Novak playing crippled and taped.

I decided on my own to limp over to the campus health office and get my foot X-rayed. The picture showed a clear crack in the outside of the fifth metatarsal bone, about halfway between the heel and little toe.

"Can't I just tape it up good and play?" I suggested to the doctor.

"The break is right where a tendon is attached," he said, shaking his head. "Unless you immobilize the foot, it cannot heal. Every step you take will prevent recovery." I told the doctor about the upcoming important series with Bradley in our second interconference, regional playoff series in four years. As Big Seven champions again, we were once more heading into postseason play. Nebraska baseball hadn't had anything like this happen for as long as anyone could remember.

"I'm sorry," the doctor said. "You wouldn't be much good to the team. This will only get worse, and you won't even be able to walk if you try to play on it." So a walking cast was put on my foot.

When I hobbled into Coach Sharpe's office to inform him of the bad news, he glanced up from his desk, his eyes rolled to the back of his head, and he threw his hands into the air. Tony turned away and looked out the window, then turned back, his face contorted with pain and disbelief.

"What happened?!" he said.

My mind raced back to St. Louis where, we were playing Parks College earlier in the season. I had sprained my ankle in a game with Missouri U., and it had been taped up. Tony had told me not to take the tape off for any reason the night before the game. The next morning my ankle was swollen and very uncomfortable, so I took the tape off and went out for a short, very careful walk, intending to put the tape right back on after my circulation rejoined me.

Waiting for a traffic light to change in the chilly morning air, I began jogging in place very carefully to keep warm. Unaware that I was drifting to the edge of the sidewalk, I came down with my foot half off the curb, painfully rolling the weakened, unsupported ankle again. My teammates had to help me back to the hotel lobby, where we met a very angry coach. I had disobeyed his instructions. I was very clearly at fault.

I was sure this memory streaked through Tony's mind as I stood there in my calf-high walking cast. But this time it was not my fault. In fact, I estimated that I had played at least four conference games in pain on a cracked bone that I had received during game action.

Nevertheless, I felt terrible. I wanted to say, maybe I can play anyway; I could still make the double play; I'll just cheat a little more toward second. But that was no good. I would still have to hobble out infield hits. I didn't quite understand why the coach was so distraught, though; he still had Bill Jensen, a fine infielder with a stronger arm than mine. I tried to think of something to cheer Tony up, but nothing came to mind. The only thing good about the moment at all was the realization that I would be missed, that I was important to the team.

There wasn't much else said at that meeting. I finally made my way out the door and went home, leaving Tony with his head in his hands.

Bradley took us out in two straight games, each by four runs. Bradley's Bill Tuttle, who two years later would go up to Detroit in the American League, went crazy and hit about .900 in the games against us and the following NCAA championship series. His batting average looked like a fielding average. I felt reasonably certain that my presence could not have overcome this, even with the end of the Big Seven Conference stats listing me tied for first in stolen bases with Lee Knox of Iowa State and Bud French of Kansas: ten in less than twenty games, some of them on bad wheels.

Now, I had to worry about McCook's reaction to my walking cast. Fortunately, I would have to keep it on for less than two weeks of the NIL season.

McCook took the news much more calmly than Tony had—maybe a little too calmly, I thought. How good was this Mickey Stubblefield, I wondered? He and Horace Garner were returning as regulars for the 1950 NIL season, and I knew Mickey was a proven second baseman as well as a tough pitcher.

I limped to my job at the *Gazette*, wrote up the games and my column, hung around with the guys. Then it was time to cut the cast off. I would be back in the lineup for the next game, I thought. The cast came off and I stared in amazement at my puny leg, which just four weeks earlier had been muscular and robust. My ankle seemed so small. I carefully put my foot on the floor and started to walk. I almost fell down. I could not support my weight up off the heel.

"I'm crippled!" I thought. "My leg has shrunk! Mickey Stubblefield now playing second base for McCook," the announcer in my mind said. I had never had worn a cast before, so the process of muscular atrophy and rebuilding was all new to me. To my great relief, it was not nearly as lengthy as I first imagined. I was soon walking carefully, then almost jogging, and finally even sprinting a little. Then I was back in the game.

You Can't Always Judge a Baseball Bum by Its Cover

Near the middle of June that summer I was walking through the Superior Hotel lobby before a game when Eddie Miller, his personable grin beaming a little wider than usual, motioned for me to follow him. "C'mere," he said. Entering the dining room behind him, I heard the sound of a piano. "Look," Eddie said, still grinning as if he had put me onto a story for my column, which he had.

Seated at the piano, with a small electric organ angled to his right, was a large man with a graying crewcut and a cigar stub in his mouth, his 240 pounds bunched in the comfortable upright position of a pianist who knew what he was doing. His strong hands and forearms hovered over the keyboard; huge fingers found notes with a majestic ease, delivering chords and melodies with a beauty and sensitivity that completely contradicted his blunt appearance.

"Who is that?" I whispered to Eddie.

"That's Superior's new right fielder, Connie Creedon," Eddie said, still grinning.

At first glance I'd thought Creedon was some club bouncer or a maintenance worker who had stopped to play the first few bars of "Heart and Soul" or "Chopsticks," but within seconds I realized we were in the presence of a very gifted and trained musician. He could play everything—classics, jazz, blues, boogie-woogie, church hymns, pop songs, opera, and ragtime—and play it without mistakes, with soul and skill, with rhythm and touch. And all without any sheet music.

Bill Gardner

"Gimme a light, Danny," Creedon said to the McCook manager, Danny Farris, who two years before had managed Superior and also knew Connie from earlier baseball times together in the Southern Association and the Providence League in Canada. Farris jumped out of his chair at this request.

"Sure I'll give you a light," he said. "I'll light that cigar all day just to keep you playing here." He looked at our team, which by now had formed a sizable audience. "Ain't he terrific?" Danny exclaimed, sounding like Creedon's agent. There was no doubt about it. He was terrific. "Play 'Stardust,'" Danny said.

Creedon shifted some levers and stops on the organ and played it as Hoagy Carmichael would have wanted it played.

"Ain't he terrific!" Farris said again, very proud of his old baseball friend.

I went over to ask Farris about this newfound genius, who destroyed all preconceived physical conceptions of an accomplished pianist. Creedon sat there looking like a "quarter-to-three" honky-tonk piano player. All the scene lacked were some empty beer mugs and cigar burns on the piano.

"He's an automobile salesman down here," Dan said, "and he sells cars just like he plays that thing." In that case, I thought, he must be making some dealer a fortune.

Creedon began to play some boogie-woogie with a walking bass and a great right hand. P. O. Karthauser got up and started jitter-bugging like a World War II canteen champion.

"Ain't he terrific?" Farris said.

Half an hour later Connie was about ready to quit, and it was time to suit up for the game.

"Before you go," Gene Dellenbach requested, "would you play 'Ave Maria'?"

Creedon played it as beautifully as I have ever heard it. Then he got up and left with Danny Farris at his side, Danny's arm proudly around his amazing and unpublicized friend's shoulder. We all just sat there quietly for a few moments. We needed a little more time before going off to baseball.

On the field at Superior that night I noticed a few other new faces. At shortstop during infield practice a lean 180-pounder with over six feet of broad-shouldered athletic quickness received a ground ball in the hole with nonchalance, planted his right foot, and dispatched the ball to first base in an easy overhand motion with a wrist whip on the end which sent the ball with almost no arc on the longest throw across the infield. I thought, wait a minute— that throw came completely across the infield in about the time my throw from second gets there. And my arm was not bad at all. This, I said to myself, bears watching.

The new shortstop threw around the bases a few more times, and I thought, this is indeed a wondrous arm! What an evening. First a genius at the piano, and now a shortstop who throws as hard as Horace Garner. And he makes it look so easy. Watching someone perform in that gifted manner on the diamond during infield practice was by itself worth the price of admission to me.

His name was Tommy Hurd, and he had come as part of an order Superior had placed with its Class B Three-I League connection in Waterloo, Iowa. Later Tommy came in to relieve, and he threw the ball right by us. His knee-high fast ball was all but invisible; at waist height you could almost catch a glimpse of it. Tom had come with, and would compile, some very impressive credentials. He arrived in Superior from Waterloo with an 18 and 11 record. In 1953, used only as a pitcher, he won eighteen games for Nashville in the Southern Association. He moved on up to the Boston Red Sox of the American League and pitched in 1954–56, winning 13, losing 10 and saving 11.

Sometimes ignorance not only is bliss but allows you the confidence that knowledge would scare out of you. If I had known what Tom Hurd had done and would later do, I might have tightened up and been a quick out. But as it was, I stood there calmly late in the game with the bases full and Tommy throwing two lasers by me. Then I fouled one, and then another. For some reason he stayed completely with the fast ball. I was a good fast ball hitter. It took some pitchers a few times around to learn that the out pitch on me was the breaking ball off the plate or the change-up.

I finally timed Tommy's fast ball and lined it directly at Connie

Creedon in right field. Breaking for first, I saw Creedon take two steps, stop, and jump as high as his 240 pounds would go while my drive rose over his glove and to the fence for a bases-clearing triple. It was especially satisfying to me because my father and mother had driven down from Lincoln to Superior (the only NIL town within reasonable driving distance for them) to see the game—the only one they would see in my six-year NIL career.

Creedon had a "Ruthian" swing and whistled a couple of line drives over me during that game. The most unusual part of his swing was the way he spun the bat in quick circles just before the pitch—like Willie Stargell, but years before Willie, of course. Creedon's windmill cranking-up was not a copy.

At second base for Superior that night was another new face, and a rugged, battling face it was. I remembered seeing Pepper Martin of the Cardinals play in a Pacific Coast League game at San Francisco in 1945, just before I went overseas. I hadn't been close enough to see Pepper's face, but everything about his "Gas House Gang" playing style and build came to mind as I watched Superior's new second baseman, Matt Sepich, also recently acquired from the Three-I League's Waterloo, Iowa, team.

One play and its consequence during that game in Superior made an impression on me which stuck. Matt hit a line drive down the third-base line, which the base umpire called foul. Matt promptly raced over to the small umpire, "Dud" Graham, screaming and jumping with objections. Highly animated, he kept on bullying the defenseless little arbitrator, who began walking, head down, toward second base to escape the abuse of this not especially tall but very muscular second baseman screaming at his heels. When I, in a moment of ill-timed umpire sympathy—of baseball-code stupidity—expressed an opinion of the call that did not agree with Sepich's, he turned and raced over to me. Puffing up to a fearsome size in rage, he told me to stay the hell out of it when he was bullying his umpires and made it clear if I ever did it again, he would very likely drag the infield with me.

Of course Matt was completely right. Even then I intuitively sensed that it was bad form to enter into a private discussion between player and umpire, though nobody had ever actually told me so. I was as surprised as anyone that I had, and wise sayings such as "Look before you leap" and that old wartime favorite "Loose lips sink ships" flashed through my mind. When I got back to our bench, Grogan, usually a very quiet guy, said, "Hey Hobe, slap some color back into your face." That caused our bench to break into uncontrollable laughter, and I, seeing the humor in it too, tried to join them, but my mouth wouldn't work.

Matt was both a piece of work and a work in progress when he played. In fact, if you'd caught his act one particularly cold night game, you might have thought his yarn was wound a little too loosely. Wearing some strange blanket garment to protest playing in the cold weather, he went to bat and lifted a home run over the right-field fence. He raced around the bases at full speed, the weird garment fluttering all the way like a ripped sail, and slid into home with all the finesse of a big kite crashing in the mud. Matt then jumped to his feet, flapping like an early flying contraption, in violent protest with the home plate umpire—who was more than confused, since he had made no call, the ball having cleared the fence in obvious fair territory, eliminating any possible play at home. After winning the "argument," Sepich ran to the next hitter, insisting that he too wear the garment for good luck, and wrestled him to the ground when he objected.

Matt was really in control of everything he did, but he was the only one who knew it. Much like P. O. Karthauser in knowing how to get the fans into the ball game, he was willing to fire all his dramatic forces into the fray for the good of the cause. To know Matt was simply to stand back and let him perform. Behind these moments of lunacy was a very competitive, talented, blue-collar baseball player of the old school.

It was starting to get light behind us as we sped westward, approaching McCook. Bob Grogan and Bob West were talking, trying to keep each other awake; every now and then I would wake up in the back seat and hear their distant, vibrating voices. I glanced at my watch. Four-fifteen and five more miles to go. Then we were in front of my house. Outside the car it seemed as if six thousand birds were awake and chirping. I picked up my gear bag and scorebook and climbed out of the car. It had suddenly become very light.

"Goodnight," Grogan said.

"Good morning," I said. I stood a moment, watching the car drive down West Fourth street, and then looked at the sunrise. I stumbled into our basement apartment and glanced again at my watch. Quarter to five. What a time to be going to bed. Grogan and West doubted they would even try, since they had to be at work very early.

Three and a half hours later I sat at the *Gazette* typewriter, trying to unscramble the scorebook and remember what had happened in the game the night before at Superior. It was tricky trying to read another person's scoring symbols, but I had to have someone else keep the stats because it was awkward to do it while playing, especially in the field.

My eyelids drooped and the pencil fell out of my hand. I picked it up and slapped myself in the face crisply with the other hand, just hard enough to sting a little and get my attention. Something's got to be done about this Superior trip, I thought. It's just too long. I slapped my cheek again as my eyelids were going down for a second time. Write the story, write the story! I thought. Write the story— tell the folks why Superior beat us again.

I didn't see Ephraim, a McCook sports fan, come in, until he folded the sports page noisily and slapped his knee with it in disgust. I looked up to see him unscrew the cap off a bottle and take a big swig.

"Hey," I said. "You can't drink in here. Mr. Strunk has rules."

"This is Hadacol," Ephraim said. "You better take a belt yourself so you can stay awake." Hadacol, a highly publicized "miracle" elixir of that time, claimed to be an herb-vitamin mixture that would not only give a person great energy and health but cure anything and everything.

Ephraim pointed to the NIL standings. "What's the matter, what's the matter, what's the matter with the team!?" he demanded. "Superior, 11 and 3; McCook, 10 and 6!" He took another nip of the famous health beverage and sank into a chair.

Several minutes later portly Ed Manley—McCook post office worker by day, NIL umpire by night—burst into the office. Hot on his trail was Superior's manager, Frank Jones, still very upset over some of Manley's calls against Superior. Six rule books fell out of Manley's pocket. As he stooped to pick them up, Jones fell over him and crashed into the wall.

"Sit down," Ephraim said. "Be seated, my friend. I would like a word with you." Frank Jones swung at Manley with a thirty-six-inch Joe DiMaggio but missed. "You be seated too, sir," Ephraim said to Jones. Manley and Jones fell into chairs, breathing heavily. Ephraim offered them the dark bottle of magic cure-all.

"You should choke up on that thirty-six-inch bat. It's too heavy for you," Manley said to Jones.

"You are an umpire, are you not?" Ephraim asked Manley.

"Yes," Manley said. "That is correct."

"I object!" Jones shouted, spilling the herb-vitamin liquid on a throw rug. The rug got up, curled itself around the nearest chair, and crushed it.

"Please," Ephraim said, "do not interrupt. Manley, what is the matter with McCook this year? Where is the championship team of 1948? What has happened to the boys? Where is my Hadacol?"

"Championship team of 1948? That was a one-time thing," Manley answered. "Look back at the box scores and see who McCook was playing. Now look at the lineups today. Do you see many of the same guys? In 1948 North Platte was McCook's cousin. Not today. Superior was a sad second-division weak sister. Not today! The lineups look like All-Star Texas, American Association, Western, Three-I League teams. McCook in 1948 was the strongest NIL team. Today the Cats are not. They are right there in the fight, but to win in the NIL today the breaks have to fall your way. And lately they haven't for McCook."

"Oh," Ephraim said, putting a heavy chair on the rug, which, the Hadacol having evaporated, had run out of strength. "Then you mean there is actually that much difference this year?"

"More," Manley said.

"How do you know, Manley?!" Jones shouted. "Who told you? You couldn't umpire a game of statue!" Jones swung again and knocked Manley for a double down the left-field line. Manley came in on the first hop to second and tossed Jones out of the game. Jones wrote a letter of apology, and enclosed two tickets to the East Ward Elementary School statue tournament. Manley bought Jones a beer.

"How's the Superior game story coming?" called a voice from the outer office. "It's awfully quiet in there."

My elbow slipped off the arm of my old swivel chair and my head dropped, snapping my neck and waking me suddenly. I strained to connect with something that would tell me where I was, what time of the day it might be, and whose voice I had just heard. It was a frightening moment of complete panic and disorientation. I turned my head and rubbed my neck, groping to come back to reality and get my bearings.

Something really had to be done about those all-night trips home from Superior.

A few days later, Mickey Stubblefield walked up to me. He seemed to be feeling fine and ready to burst with some announcement.

"What's on your mind, Mick?" I said.

"I didn't used to be healthy. I was just a little puny man," Mickey said. "I weighed only 113 pounds and I was always tired and run down. I was nervous, irritable, and my curve ball wouldn't break. I would fall down when I tried to run to first base, and I would hit myself in the head when I tried to swing a bat. I was very unhappy. Then I tried Hadacol, and now look at me. I've gained two hundred pounds. I'm a big huge man with muscles. My curve ball is breaking. I can go nine innings or fifteen, and I hit line drives over the fence. I feel fine. I can run all the way to first base, and I don't hit myself with the bat anymore."

"Stay away from those Hadacol ads, Mick," I said laughing, as he went on down the sidewalk.

Later, I told Eddie Miller about Mickey's funny testimony for Hadacol, the miracle tonic that was even publicized in three-column ads on the sports page of the *Gazette*. I laughed again, remembering Mickey's enthusiastic delivery.

"He really drinks that stuff, you know," Eddie said, his face as serious as he was ever able to make it.

The McCook Cats were not at the top of the NIL standings midway through the 1950 season, and there were rumblings of discontent throughout the little Red Willow County town. The trouble with handing baseball fans such a dazzling product as an NIL championship overnight, after they'd become accustomed to the cellar, was that they expected the same product, or better, from then on. But there could hardly be a "better." We'd delivered that 1948 championship to the win-starved McCook fans with a 17 and 3 season of NIL dominance, taking the Shaughnessy playoffs in five straight games and posting a final season total record of 36 wins and just 5 losses. It was impossible even to equal such a startling feat, since all the other NIL teams had plunged with total resources into the outside recruitment program and brought near parity to the league.

Nevertheless, McCook fans had become extremely fond of winning, and when the Cats could not provide wins with the automatic regularity of 1948, the natives were restless, even ugly. Suddenly, manager Danny Farris became the problem, and whispers of running him out of town rose to an ominous rumble.

Farris tried to think of ways to bolster his job security. He decided we needed some serious positive promotion, including help from me in my column at the *Gazette*. The team was called together for a photo session in the rough outfield with the scoreboard behind us at Fairgrounds Ballpark. "Come on, hustle it up!" Farris snapped, the strain of the situation showing on his face. Mickey Stubblefield, Horace Garner, and Ed Van Nordheim were gathered around a camera. "Come on, you Hoosiers," Farris said, "when I say out on the field by six, I don't mean six-thirty!" Danny thought he was still a marine drill sergeant, which he'd once told somebody he had been. The thought of losing another game was weighing heavily on his mind.

Cletus Brooks of Brooks Studio adjusted his camera on the tripod as Stubblefield practiced his pitching motion, trying to hold it with one foot in the air. "How's that?" Mickey said, then lost his balance and almost fell on his head. Brooks went over to him to see if something couldn't be done.

"Put that bottle of Hadacol away, Mickey," Van Nordheim said. "Do you want the fans to think we're all a bunch of drunks?" Mickey actually did not have his Hadacol with him. He had left it at home.

"Yeah," P. O. Karthauser said. "That's all we need with the way we been playing lately."

Van Nordheim, Stubblefield, and Bill Gardner got together on the mound for a picture of the pitching staff. Ed pushed an enormous wad of tobacco into his cheek, and assumed a relaxed stance, and Mickey was trying to pose again without falling down.

"Somebody hold on to Van Nordheim," P. O. said. "He's going to tip over with all that tobacco in his cheek."

"Hurry up and shoot the picture!" Mickey said. "I can't hold my foot in the air much longer." Brooks finally snapped a few shots of the mound staff.

"All right," Farris said, "let's get some hitters over here with bats."

Donnie Hays, 145-pound sparkplug third baseman, picked up three bats and started toward the camera.

"Sluggers?" he said. "Did someone call my name?"

"Hitters, I said," Farris snapped. "Eddie, you and Horace and Grogan get over there with some bats."

Then Brooks wanted a group picture. Everyone closed in, and the ones in the front row took their positions on one knee.

"Hey," Gene Dellenbach said, "we can't sit here. There's big red ants all over."

"That's all right," Van Nordheim said. "When they bite P. O., they'll die."

"Or break their pinchers," Mickey said.

"Hey, Farris," Bob West called, "I hear you're a big wheel now. A Farris wheel."

"All right, you clowns," Farris said, "lay off the wise stuff. Let's get serious here."

Brooks almost had everything under control. Finally he moved to his camera and took hold of the black bulb.

"Don't say anything funny, Horace," Mickey said. "I want to look mean this time."

Some time later the picture was taken, and everyone began walking off the field except Mickey, who was trying to stick a baseball to a bat with a big bunch of bubble gum, for a bunting photo.

While the quality and cost of NIL baseball were soaring to unexpected new heights, one aspect of the league, sadly, was neglected and fell behind. That, by general agreement, was the umpiring. Since I had included complaints about it in my column, I felt obligated to present the umpires' side as well, especially after speaking with my umpiring friend and fellow McCook citizen, Ed Manley, and finding out that he was a little hurt and offended by the criticism. I gave the NIL umpires' view through the following spoof, which I slipped into one of my "Sports Haze" columns:

It happened just outside the Post Office. I was on my way to mail a letter when I got it. I heard a voice.

"Draw!" it shouted. I wheeled, whipped out my Wood-clinched Ebony copy pencil, and drew. But I was too late. Ed "Ringo" Manley beat me with his indicator, and called a third strike. I dropped to one knee, clasping my wound.

"Why, Ed, why?" I gasped.

"I been meaning to write you a letter," Ringo said, dusting ashes from his cigar, "both you and Don Lindstrom. You both been writing things about us umpires."

"But I was writing about calling the plays too soon," I wheezed. Everything was getting blurred. "I never saw you call one too soon."

"You had it coming, kid," Ringo said, checking his indicator. "You talk about the umpiring not being up to the ball being played. You guys are getting paid enough for what you do. Do you know what we get?"

"No," I whispered, rolling over on my side.

"Ten bucks a game," Ringo said. "You can get that much for going around and refereeing any small high school basketball game. Thirty minutes of work. And here you spend two to three hours out there and take all kinds of abuse for the same thing." Manley applied a tourniquet to my neck and things began to clear up. "It is hardly worth it. If they want quality umpiring, they should pay for it."

"You're right," I said, suddenly feeling much better. "I didn't realize how it was from your side. The umpires are calling 10 dollars worth of baseball, at least."

I got to my feet, shook hands with Manley and mailed my letter. Ringo returned to his job at the Post Office, and peace was restored between players and umpires for the day.

Walking about in the McCook town park with my thoughts one night that summer, which I often did (in those years it could be done without fear of being accosted by strangers or questioned by the police), I was roused from my reverie by someone crying at the other side of the park. I listened, concerned that maybe this person needed help. The sobbing voice moved unseen in the darkness. It sounded like a young woman or a teenage girl, walking and crying with all the tears of young, painful discovery or rejection. She was not calling for help. She seemed only to need to cry, to release a flood of disappointment and emotional pain without concern for the world around her. So I remained at a distance, listening until the weeping trailed off and was gone, and I wondered for a few moments about the cause of her grief. Then I slowly walked home, realizing that my loneliness in the night was nothing next to that immense, solitary despair.

As I sat down in the little basement apartment in Mrs. Fagan's home, still absorbed with my thoughts from the park, the phone rang.

"I've got to talk to you, Hobe," a troubled voice said. It was Danny Farris, our manager. I knew there was some dissatisfaction from the Baseball Board with the way our team was playing, and I thought this call might be about that problem.

"Okay," I said. "Go ahead."

"No," Danny said, "I mean talk. I'm down at Modrell's Café. I'll wait for you."

"Dan," I protested, "do you know what time it is? It's almost midnight, and I'm getting ready to go to bed."

"I've got to talk to somebody," Farris said. "I'll wait for you here."

I had learned to recognize when somebody really needed to talk. Loneliness was something I knew about. Dan Farris, a lean, highstrung thirty-four-year-old, was one of the purest baseball bums I would ever meet. His rapidly thinning brown hair perched above a permanently stress-wrinkled forehead, and his piercing blue eyes blazed with anxiety as he drifted from one baseball job to another—now a manager for Superior, now a manager for McCook—wearing his big Cincinnati warmup jacket, which we assumed he had obtained while pitching for the Reds. I really didn't know where he was from, or if he had actually played for Cincinnati or ever even pitched. Dan had a way of talking himself into baseball jobs. His trouble was holding on to them. He looked like an illustration for Satchel Paige's motto, "Don't look back—something might be gaining on you." Dan moved about as if pursued by invisible hellhounds, on a leash but slowly gaining on him.

I found him in a booth at Modrell's, sitting with a cigarette and a cup of black coffee, staring across the room. I sat down opposite him and ordered coffee with cream and sugar. He said nothing at first, but at last he spoke.

"I thought all the decent stuff went down the drain during the war," he said, not interrupting his thoughts to greet me. "I thought the war made tramps out of all of them." He sipped his coffee and peered through his cigarette smoke. "I didn't think there were any good ones left. They all went down the sewer with the trash during the war."

I thought I had a sense of what he was talking about, but I said nothing, certain that it would become clearer as Danny went on.

"I met a woman," Dan continued, "here in McCook, who didn't go down the drain. She's decent, she's like the women were before the war. And I think I love her. All I can do is think of her. She's too good for me—she doesn't see that now, but she will. What do I have to give her? Where am I going with my life? What have I to show for my life? I never thought I would meet a woman again who would make me think like this. I'm thirty-four years old. What do I have to show for those years? She comes from a decent Christian family. She has brothers and sisters who are decent too. They all got through the war. What do I have to give her?"

I sipped my coffee and waited to speak. It didn't seem like the time yet.

"I think about her a lot," Farris continued. "She's the best thing that ever happened to me, and when she really knows me, I'll lose her. What would a fine woman like that want with a baseball bum like me?"

Not yet, I thought. No questions. No suggestions. Just listen.

"I didn't need any woman before," Danny went on, "just once in a while to get my ashes hauled. I never found one before I wanted to be with all the time. You know what I'm talking about? Did you ever feel that way about a woman?"

Now, I thought. But don't take too long.

"Yeah," I said, "a couple of times. I know what you're saying—"

Farris didn't hear me. His strained, wrinkled forehead sheltered two glassy blue eyes that stared blankly through the café's big window glass. We sat there a long time, Dan saying something every now and then about the war and its women.

It was late when we paid the check and went outside. I said goodnight to Danny as he walked away, hunched in his big Cincinnati jacket, a cigarette stuck on his lip.

Later that month the McCook Baseball Board fired Danny Farris and designated Ed Van Nordheim to take the Cats home in the stretch. There are only rumors of what happened to Farris.

I think things were known in the NIL that were never told to me, because people never knew when something they said might appear in my column. In retrospect, I feel certain that if the league officials wanted to keep something out of the papers (the NIL was getting enough bad publicity from Bill Madden of the *Hastings Tribune* and Walt Charlesworth of the *Holdrege Citizen*), they kept me from knowing about it. Though I have a strong feeling those hounds of hell were somehow involved, I have never heard anything from a reliable source about the disappearance of Danny Farris, so what I did hear remains just rumor.

The same must be said in regard to Connie Creedon's brief but memorable visit to Superior and exit from the NIL.

Nor did I ever find out who the crying girl was, or what caused her great sobbing.

Ed Van Nordheim, reluctant midseason replacement for Dan Farris, was another of those over-six-foot NIL pitchers. Ed also looked as if he'd missed very few meals, and his very dry wit made him the team's funny man. And he was a left-hander.

In one game at Superior, though Ed seemed to have good stuff, that night he couldn't get any of it by that great lineup of Creedon, Hurd, Stickney, Sepich, Heim, and Wonka. Everything Ed delivered came back a double, a triple, or a run-scoring single. He stood there and watched the ball streak toward the fence between outfielders and now and then sail over it. He shook his head in bewilderment as the runners crossed the plate.

In about the seventh inning one of the Knights smashed a drive over the head of Eddie Miller in center field. Miller chased the ball down and relayed to Grogan, whose perfect throw to home caught the sliding runner for the third out. Completely exhausted and discouraged, Van Nordheim still had a smile in him as he trudged to the dugout. "I've finally found a way to get them out of there," he said, throwing his glove down in the corner of the dugout. "I'll pitch to their power, and we'll cut them off at home."

Tommy O'Connor, a new catcher imported from Canada for North Platte, was a very good left-handed hitter, had a great arm, and was fast. He was also good-looking, persuasive, and engaging—a perfect salesman. On one memorable night he did a great selling job in calling balls and strikes for the umpire. Some catchers have a way of coming up out of the crouch and yelling "yeah!" or "strike" as they catch a pitch, and firing it down to third for the "around the horn" strikeout celebration. Many times this works, and the umpire looks at his indicator and rings up strike three.

O'Connor was doing a masterful job in this role that night, and the McCook dugout was smoldering at the cagey receiver's apparent control of the plate umpire. P. O. Karthauser became very upset and began yelling critical and insulting things at the umpire. The rest of our bench joined P. O. in suggesting that the umpire get control of the game again. Ed Van Nordheim, who was pitching that game, topped everything when he shouted to O'Connor as the catcher faked a throw down to first to pick off a runner.

"Don't throw that ball down there, catch," Ed warned. "You might lose your indicator!"

The firing of Danny Farris and our uneasiness from losing games we shouldn't have—plus the feeling that something was missing that year, despite our collection of fine players—left us in anything but midseason form in my third NIL summer. Even with Van Nordheim's light and humorous touch, things were still a little tense as we drove into Goodland, Kansas, for a non-league exhibition game.

When we walked onto the field, I wondered if we were in the right place. About ten yards foul of the first-base line was a hole about six by eighteen feet and some three feet deep. Around it was piled all the dirt that had been in it, so that its general appearance was that of a small dam project. I found out later they were going to put a dugout in there.

Ed Van Nordheim çame up to me. He was either smiling or the tobacco in his mouth was stretching his face.

"You should have been here sooner," he said, looking over at the manmade canyon. "I just pitched my way out of a hole."

"Hey, Ed," someone said, pointing to the huge, lighted water tower looming directly behind the grandstand. "This is big time. Look at the size of that press box."

"Yeah," Ed agreed. "There must be sportswriters from all over the country here tonight."

We were almost late for the game, so we started warming up right away. I was warming up Dave Garland when I noticed something going on over at the hole. Van Nordheim was standing on top of the pile of dirt, which sloped about 45 degrees down to the bottom, trying to get the sign from P. O. Karthauser, who was down in the hole with his mask on. Ed wound up, kicked, and stepped four feet down in mock slow motion, lobbing the ball to Karthauser. Then he climbed back up, looking around excitedly.

"Boy," he said, "have I got stuff off this mound!"

There was a good crowd that night, with many of the fans along the fences in parked cars, and when the side was retired or the hometown boys made a good play, they honked all their horns in applause. I don't remember what we did to keep the catchers and first basemen from falling into the ditch on foul pop flies, but I do remember that the clowning around before the game at Goodland, Kansas, broke the tension that had been preventing our club from performing as we could. We went on to have a winning season.

But Superior, continuing to overpower the NIL, won the championship of 1950 with possibly the most "professional" semi-pro team seen in the league's eight-year Golden Age. The Knights took the title with 23 wins and 7 losses (and won 32 of a total of 42 league and non-league games) in a year when all the teams were near their peak, thanks to heavy outside recruitment. The total number of years of professional baseball experience represented by this Knights team may have topped that of any other one team in the history of the NIL.

Starting with manager Floyd Stickney, the minor league credits of the 1950 NIL winners seemed almost to disqualify the Knights from semi-pro status. Floyd was with Worthington in the Class D Western League in 1940, with Albany in the Class D Georgia-Florida League in 1941, and with Mobile and Decatur, Illinois, of the Class B Three-I League in 1942.

Shortstop/pitcher Tommy Hurd, with possibly the strongest arm in the NIL, had compiled an 18-and-11 record at Waterloo in the Three-I League. From Waterloo he'd been sold to Memphis in the Double A Southern Association but was unhappy with his contract and decided that working at a job in Superior and getting paid well to play NIL ball there for a couple of years was financially better. Second baseman Matt Sepich had also had an outstanding record in Waterloo; he too liked the combination money temporarily offered by playing ball for Superior and holding a town job. Pitcher Mel

Nicolai, yet another member of the "Waterloo Purchase," had an outstanding slider before they called it that.

Casey Wonka was brought in from Class D ball in Miami, Oklahoma. Big Connie Credon had been playing pro ball in Galt, Ontario, Canada. George Dockins was a former big league pitcher; he'd had an 8-and-6 record with the St. Louis Cardinals in 1945 and had seen some mound action for the Brooklyn Dodgers in 1947. Duane White, Jim McMahon, Gene Graves, Merrill McDonald, and Val Heim were all well-traveled and excellent semi-pro players.

It was little wonder that the Knights took the championship, but the Cats got a taste of revenge in the Shaughnessy playoffs. About midnight in early September 1950 the crowded M&E Café in McCook buzzed with conversation, and the clinking of coffee spoons cut through the jukebox strains of Patti Paige singing "My Happiness." As I walked toward the counter to pay my bill, I noticed some familiar faces, almost unrecognizable behind new beards grown for Superior's "Western Days."

"Don't they have any razor blades down at Superior?" I said. Matt Sepich wheeled around, turned his blazing eyes on me, and made an animated gesture of despair.

"You lucky bastards!" he screamed, throwing an elbow over the back of the booth.

"Lucky!?" I said, returning his scream but somewhat muting it. "A five-hit shutout lucky!?"

"You heard me!" Sepich's scream was slightly softer. I laughed.

"Surely you must be joking," I said. I looked at Superior's manager, Floyd Stickney, his cheeks puffed with chicken-fried steak, who smiled a hello. Then I glanced back at Sepich, greatly resembling a lumberjack with his new beard.

"I hope you guys have your fire trucks with you when you come down Tuesday," he declared, "because we're going to burn up those bases. We're going to set fire to them with all the times we are going to score, and you will be the fire."

Stickney smiled as if to say, "That is my second baseman talking, but I tend to agree with him, if not in those exact words." Sepich took a drink of coffee, wiped his beard, held up a finger for attention, and continued: "We're going to run up that score so high you guys are going to be sorry you ever got in the playoffs in the first place," he said with finality. He wasn't through, however. "Garland is the only pitcher you guys have that can beat us," he added. "We'll knock out every other pitcher you have!" I muttered something to Stickney about doing something to help build up his second baseman's self confidence. "We're going to take three straight now. We're going to beat you so bad you'll wish you never got lucky this time," he concluded.

Sepich stroked his beard, gleamed like Mephistopheles himself, and waited for the chance to deliver another verbal blitzkrieg. Over in the corner Dave Garland stood by the pinball machine behind his small son, who was pulling the marble shooter. The elder Garland's arm might have been a little weary. It deserved a rest after throwing a five-hit shutout against the hardest-hitting club in the NIL that season. It would be several years before the younger Garland could understand just what a fine job of pitching his dad had turned in that night. I located Jack Baxter, who was temporarily sharing the apartment at Mrs. Fagan's house with Don and me, and went home.

In spite of Matt Sepich's assurances of catastrophic arson on the diamond, and without bringing our fire trucks, McCook defeated Superior for the third straight game, thereby eliminating the powerful 1950 NIL champion Knights in the first round of the Shaughnessy playoffs. Mickey Stubblefield came into the game in the third and pitched outstanding one-hit relief to post a 4-to-1 victory.

As for me, I finished the summer strong, hitting .329 and fielding .986. That should hold my position secure until the next season, I thought as I packed up to go to the Chicago Art Institute on a one-year scholarship. It had been awarded at the end of my senior year at the University of Nebraska, Duard Laging had informed me, for my hard work and artistic potential.

Windy City Blues

Peering down from a challenging tier of entrance steps, a pair of enormous stone lions stood guard over the Chicago Art Institute in the fall of 1950. Michigan Avenue traffic honked and rumbled in businesslike indifference past the impressive sentries as the cold wind off Lake Michigan sent an early morning chill through my lightweight jacket. Inside the heavy entrance doors and down the long and confusing hallways, the open doors of endless classrooms exposed half-finished canvases of the human figure, their various approaches ranging from the realism of Degas, Rembrandt, and Daumier to the decorative excellence of Matisse.

The quality of all the varying approaches to the nude model was stunning and almost intimidating. Gathered in this nationally respected center for developing artists were students from many places outside the Chicago area as well as locally encouraged talent. They all knew there was very little mediocrity in attendance. If I had traveled to Chicago puffed up with thoughts of my own art excellence, it took only a few minutes of looking into classrooms to bring me down to size.

I had never been in a class that used nude models before Chicago. Once past the initial impact of the completely disrobed female, I was surprised how casual and familiar the whole experience became with only a few minutes of work at the easel. Very soon it was just another day at the office, nothing to get excited about.

The Art Institute models came in all sizes and shapes. They were paid very well, so there was never any trouble filling the positions.

George Lebedz

In Professor Weighart's painting class our first model was a young woman who could have stepped right out of a Rubens painting—fleshy, languidly robust, a symphony of curves designed to give the artist ample direction and inspiration. The exact opposite was the tiny, wiry woman in Professor Philbrick's drawing class. Tipping the scales at probably seventy-five or eighty pounds, this bundle of nervous energy was hard pressed to hold a pose for more than a few seconds. Her wispy, angular frame was devoid of curves, but it could not be overlooked that what Mother Nature had neglected to endow her with in womanly flesh, she had overcompensated for with hair.

Apparently aware of her lack of fleshy charms, this sprite of a woman carried on a continuous chatter with the reluctant students in what seemed to be an effort at diversion. I found it annoying and looked forward to the end of each class. Professor Philbrick, a small man of more than considerable age, would spend a good part of the class period out of the room. I think he not only tired of being on his feet but also grew weary of the model's incessant chatter.

Philbrick had one dominant theory of drawing the figure. In any pose, standing, sitting, or prone, he could see a leaf shape surrounding the model, one side curved, one basically straight. If the curved side of the leaf began in the top left corner of the paper and swung to the lower right, that leaf was said to be "left-right." You drew a very light leaf outline, and then you began stating your case with the figure inside this shape. When he reentered the room to see how we were doing, he would say, "Left-right, or right-left?" repeating it as he moved among the individual drawings.

On one particular day I was having a bad time getting good results. Our model had been talking all period, and the class bell was due to ring. I could not distinguish the curved side of the leaf from the straight, and "left-right, right-left" was not evident to me with the nervous, thin, constantly moving and talking bushy object we were forced to draw. Professor Philbrick worked his way through the rows of easels and stopped at mine.

"Oh, no. No, no. Right-left, left-right? Right-left, left-right?"

"I know, I know!" I snapped, surprised at the volume of my irritated voice. "I know what to do! I just can't get it today!" Shocked by my own angry outburst, I sat red-faced, feeling the sidewise stares of the more controlled students.

"Oh, a tough guy?" Philbrick said. "I know you tough guys. Okay, tough guy," and he walked away to another student.

The end-of-class bell rang. As I folded up my tablet and my paint box, I saw Professor Philbrick just going out the door. I caught up with him in the hallway and apologized for my outburst. When he looked up at me, I realized that he was even smaller and older than I first thought.

"You have a photographic eye," he said. "Loosen up a little." A smile appeared on his tough, tired face, which suddenly looked to me like the worn face of an ex-boxer, and he winked. "Go out and find a girl. Have some fun." Then he put on his old felt hat and his raincoat and stepped lightly down the hallway, tapping the tip of his umbrella on the echoing marble floor. In my mind I saw him about fifty years earlier, bobbing, weaving, and jabbing lightly in the corner of a ring, waiting for his flyweight opponent to come out with the bell. "Right-left, left-right. Right-left, left-right."

Professor Weiner, who taught sculpture, was a very easygoing, small, stocky man of forty-some years who actually seemed to enjoy teaching. He would sit comfortably in a chair in the middle of the class and make observations, getting up once in a while to inspect our work more closely. One day he said to a student who was having trouble with his clay figure, "Go up and touch her if you are confused. Sometimes you have to feel the form because the light flattens things out."

I must admit the thought had crossed my mind ever since this particular model had slipped out of her robe, but I never thought I would be encouraged to follow my hormonal impulses by the instructor. This was a little beyond my range of action, however, and I kept my physical distance, as I had done so many times in my life.

The stout little German painting instructor, Professor Weighart, also spent considerable time out of the classroom, letting his students work quietly at their own particular pace. When he did come back into class, he would stroll about looking at the paintings with his hand on his chin and making brief comments such as "Oh, please, not so much blue." In fact, I heard that particular request so often that I felt sure Mr. Weighart had been overexposed to the color blue somewhere in his life and would just as soon not see it on the palette.

One evening at home I decided to draw a cartoon. The idea had been around for a few days, and I just had to put it on paper. I drew an awkward-looking student, his hair hanging down in his eyes, standing in front of a huge canvas. Professor Weighart (I was a good cartoonist, and the likeness was easy to see) stood in his painting smock behind the student, who had completely covered the canvas in blue, the paint running down in pools on the floor, dripping from his nose, and smudged all over his face and clothes and hands. The rest of the drawing was in black and white, so blue was the only color on the cartoon. The caption in the balloon over Weighart said: "Oh please, not so much blue."

That afternoon, making a point to be the last student out of class, I slipped up to the bulletin board and thumbtacked the cartoon at good viewing height.

The next day when I came into class, there was a warmth among the usually isolated and serious students, a hint of a communal humor on their faces, here and there an audible chuckle. Since I had never felt this glow of suppressed laughter before in the class, I thought it must have been the cartoon. Delighted with my ability to bring some humor into the room, I began painting, trying to act as I had every other day, quiet, serious, and businesslike. One student came over to me. I did not know his name. I had never even spoken to him, but I knew the broad grin on his face must have something to do with the new addition to the bulletin board.

"You did that, didn't you?" he said. He seemed genuinely delighted. I couldn't keep back a smile and nodded, yes. I was aware that some of the other students were watching us. It was one of those little moments when I felt extremely satisfied and happy. As I began to paint, I thought, "But how did they know it was mine?" I had never demonstrated that I could do anything but paint, as we all did in class. Still, it was a fine, though puzzling, moment that day at the Chicago Art Institute. I felt I had made some kind of breakthrough, some warm social contact in a daily atmosphere usually so large and impersonal.

One lunch period in the cafeteria a woman's voice called out my name. I turned and saw Ellie Stahl, classmate from the University of Nebraska. Ellie had always been an attractive girl, though somewhat shy and distant, but that day she looked unusually radiant and seemed exceptionally happy to see me. We began talking, and I thought it was wonderful to have found someone I had known before. My mind quickly began planning ways for us to get together. She seemed surprised and pleased that I too had come all the way from Nebraska to take classes at the Art Institute.

I couldn't get over how Ellie's personality had changed, how open and sparkling she was, with a new self-confidence and security. Cautiously, I let myself enter into optimism after days of loneliness and quiet classroom work. I think I was actually smiling when I noticed another person sitting down at the table with a tray of food.

"Hobe," Ellie said, "I'd like you to meet my husband." She continued to talk, smiling happily, telling me his name and other things. I saw her mouth forming words but heard little as the sounds became swallowed up in the sudden, numbing din of the big Art Institute cafeteria.

I sought escape from the impersonal and unemotional business of big-city life by attending the foreign film theater on Michigan Avenue, where I would involve myself with Jean Gabin and Simone Signoret's romantic meetings above subtitles and bottles of wine. These hours of dimly lit drama assured me that somewhere lonely people were actually making human contact with each other, if only on the movie screen.

One day in late April 1951, when the cold wind off Lake Michigan actually paused briefly to allow spring's warmth to be felt around the Art Institute, I didn't feel like drawing stick figures with a lot of hair, so I played hooky and went to Wrigley Field to watch the Cubs play the Cardinals. Stan Musial, Marty Marion, and Red Schoendienst were there for my first ever major league baseball game. I attended my second soon after and saw "Minnie" Minosa, in his first major league at-bat connect for a home run to dead center over the 410-foot marker in Comiskey Park. The White Sox, with Chico Carrasquel and young Nellie Fox, were playing Cleveland, and Al Rosen hit one of the hardest line-drive home runs to left field I have ever seen. A few months earlier I had stood on the October sidewalks in front of an appliance store on State Street and watched the magic of television bring me images of the 1950 World Series with the surprising no-name "Whiz Kids" from Philadelphia.

Another afternoon in late April of that second semester at the Art Institute I passed an open classroom door and glanced in, as was my habit, to size up some of the drawings on the easels. The model sitting in a chair on an elevated platform at the back of the room caught my eye, and I stopped, transfixed by the most physically attractive woman I had seen in Chicago. She sat like a queen, relaxed but proud, her dark hair framing a face of classic, confident beauty.

Suddenly aware that someone was in the doorway, she looked directly at me without moving her head. I don't know how long that moment of eye contact lasted, but it held me motionless. It was not the tired, bored look so many models get after holding long poses. Nor was it a denigrating "what are *you* looking at?" stare. It was out of the realm of the usual reaction when artist casually or accidentally meets the eye of model. She did not look away. Her eyes seemed to become a bit wider, but she showed no inclination to blush. I think she understood that I was paying attention to her because she was a lovely woman in all physical respects. It was a look disconnected from the usual academic examination, but I sensed she did not mind this. I even thought she reflected a certain biological interest in me.

I don't know how long I was there. I'm sure it was only a few seconds. I remember trying to appear totally professional, and I was glad I was carrying my paint box so that she could see I was a legitimate student. Then I turned and continued on down the hall.

A few days later I saw her sitting outside at lunch hour, watching a pickup ball game. She was with a good-looking guy, and as I sat down a few yards to her left, pretending to watch the game, I glanced over several times to see if she seemed to be having a good time.

The thought of her had almost gone from my mind when at the train station a week or so later I glanced down the ramp and saw about ten yards away a tall young woman reading a paperback book. Blood rushed to my neck, as it had an annoying habit of doing in exciting or crisis situations. I was almost but not quite certain it was the same person. There couldn't be two like her. Now was my chance to talk with her, I thought. What if it was someone else? So what? You say you're sorry, you made a mistake. But what do I say to start a conversation? "Excuse me, aren't you the beautiful nude model I couldn't take my eyes off that day in the doorway?" What a line! That should sweep her off her feet! She probably wouldn't go out with me anyway. She's got a big good-looking guy who looks like he has money and could take her places. I was bringing my lunch in a brown paper bag and living on a tight budget.

I mentally kicked myself. Why hadn't I gotten a part-time job and saved some money so I could take her over on the Northside where I'd discovered that great Chicago-style Dixieland jazz band? The same Floyd O'Brien was playing trombone who'd been a member of the history-making Austin High Gang in 1926 with Jimmy McPartland, Frankie Teschemaker, and Bud Freeman. I could impress her with stories of that exciting period of jazz development. Bix Beiderbecke and Louis Armstrong used to come to the White City Dance Hall to listen to those boys, who "all tried to play like Bix" but, as Armstrong and "Doc" Cheatham said, "none of them could."

Floyd O'Brien was really one of the few longtime survivors of the bathtub-gin Roaring Twenties. He and the Austin High Gang had been playing the year I was born. I remembered the beautiful muted trombone solo Floyd had recorded in the early 1930s on "Tennessee Twilight," regarded by jazz historians as a classic. And there on the Northside of Chicago in 1951 I had sat next to him between sets and tried to catch some conversation, possibly some priceless words of that time when jazz history was being made. Floyd, slumping back in the booth, had spoken to the trumpet player. I leaned in to listen. "I can't get rid of this goddamn cold," he said. "I feel like hell tonight." I thought, playing trombone with a bad cold must be a miserable thing to have to do, especially if it was a sinus cold. I was reminded of the frailty of even legends—perhaps especially legends.

My mind snapped back quickly to business at the train station. I was going to go over to her. I rapidly tried to get my approach plan together. Somehow I would work out the finance problems if she said she would go out with me. I started, then stopped to gather confidence. Suddenly her train came. It was not mine. She stepped aboard, and it took her away.

As I had so many times before in my life, I thought, "Oh, well, there's always tomorrow." But there wasn't. It was the last time I ever saw the Model Queen of the Chicago Art Institute.

Fred Wells

The North Platte Years

As the Chicago Art Institute year wound down in the spring of 1951, I wrote to the McCook Baseball Board that I would be a little late because the semester was running longer than expected. McCook wrote back: nothing personal, just business, but since I would be missing a number of early games, things had changed, and they had gone ahead and hired another second baseman. No "it's been wonderful," no "thanks for your great contributions to our overnight success," not even "we hated to have to do this, and we'll miss your clutch play around Shaughnessy playoff time."

This came as a bit of a shock, and it also angered me because it gave me very little time to make other contacts. I wasted no time, however, in telling the rest of the NIL I was available. North Platte shot back a letter saying they could use my services, since they were doing some extensive overhauling. I was relieved and happy because I'd been afraid all the teams would be set so late in the spring.

I packed up, waved goodbye to my Uncle Macklin and Aunt Marjorie Thomas and their two small sons, Michael and Evan, who had so graciously put up with me in their Chicago home for two semesters, charging me only for my share of the groceries. I boarded the train and headed west. Next stop, North Platte, home of Buffalo Bill Cody and of an NIL team definitely on the way up.

A few weeks later the cool gray June sky dampened the quiet Sand Hills town of North Platte with an intermittent and melancholy drizzle. From a counter stool in the small café I watched the small drops mark street puddles with tiny splashes. Hunched over a cup of coffee and smoking a cigarette—a new and health-destroying habit I had picked up while fighting loneliness in Chicago—I was feeling depressed even before someone dropped a few coins into the jukebox and caused Eddie Arnold to sing "Tie Me to Your Apron Strings Again." After that, Eddie went on to cheer me up further with "Born to Lose." My day was off to a great start.

I was now playing second base for the North Platte Plainsmen, and though this town of fourteen thousand was considerably larger than McCook, on that chilly, wet day it seemed even more remote and lifeless. Waiting in the barbershop, reading some back issues of the *North Platte Telegraph-Bulletin*, I had caught an article about myself.

"Hobe Hays," the news item read, "former Cat infielder and more recently of Chicago University, is expected to arrive in North Platte soon enough to be in the lineup at second base. . . . He'll have to do some fancy hitting too, if he is to hold to the pace of his predecessor, Doug Duffy, who left for summer school in Colorado." (Duffy had hit 13 for 29, to bat .448.) Now that's what I call making a newcomer feel relaxed and right at home, I thought.

I felt alone because I was starting over again. It was 1951, my fourth year in the NIL, and I was aware that though this was a new beginning it brought none of the thrill and anticipation of my first year at McCook in 1948. It was simply a new location for doing a job called "baseball." I didn't even know most of the players here, the recruitment turnover had been so rapid. I didn't have a day job yet, either, and my options in Buffalo Bill Cody's town did little to lift my spirits.

The rain began coming down harder. It would rain for most of the month of June, and at times we thought we would never get a game in before the summer was over. Hank Williams was now singing, "No Letter Today," so I ordered a chicken-fried steak to try and pick things up a little. This would be a hard year for the NIL, a real test of survival, because gate receipts were being washed away but expensive players still had to be paid. The best thing about 1951 so far was that if we could ever get a dry day, we believed we could field one of the most powerful teams the league had seen yet.

Having just come from a year at the Chicago Art Institute, where I walked every day among paintings in the permanent collection by Toulouse Lautrec, Pablo Picasso, Paul Gauguin, and other free spirits, I, in the independent tradition of Henry David Thoreau, had rented a small, isolated cabin eight miles south of North Platte to be with nature and my creative juices.

I honestly thought this would be great for a summer, but after only a week or two I was thinking, what the hell am I doing out here? I'm not some weird hermit. I'm not ready to seek seclusion from the human race, or even the rat race. I haven't even put my spikes in the starting blocks. I haven't found my perfect mate—I'm not even involved with an imperfect one—and I'm not going to find her out here. I certainly have a better chance of locating her in town. To bring any object of my affection out to my romantic lair, I first have to locate the object. I'm not getting any painting done, and I haven't a clue what to write about. And at night it's a little scary out here.

Listening to the birds and the night sounds, for the first time I became acutely aware of how important people were to me in the scheme of things. The day I finished out my short lease and eagerly drove back to town, I found pitcher Angelo Ossino sitting alone having lunch. We talked for a long time, and the dull, private ache of loneliness slowly eased away. The timeless healing powers of honest human communication had worked once more.

It had been my good fortune to work with Bob Grogan for four seasons at the University of Nebraska, two summers with Sandy Silverio's Goetz team in Lincoln, and three NIL seasons at McCook. You couldn't ask for any better working conditions. Now I would begin teaming up with a new shortstop who, I had been hearing, was as good as Grogan. This remained to be seen. His name was George Lebedz, and he was fresh from the Lincoln Athletics in the Class A Western League, where he turned double plays with Nelson "Nellie" Fox. As it turned out, by the end of 1953 I'd had six years in the NIL with the two best shortstops in that league, possibly in a few other leagues in the Midwest.

It was a pleasure doing business in the NIL. Life on the diamond was good, if not particularly exciting anymore, and I did actually look forward to each game. The time on the field was when I felt most alive, where I belonged. It was the time between games I had to do something about. There was no nice sportswriting job for me at the *Telegraph-Bulletin*, as there had been at the *Gazette*, and in my off-the-field life a low-grade anxiety was fermenting. My simple and static existence in North Platte was brewing a feeling of being left behind in a state of unproductive loss, of no advancement, no plan.

While I waited for my life plan to reveal itself, I accepted a short-term job mopping down the public swimming pool after it closed, even on the nights when we played a game, home or away. Concluding a good evening of baseball by driving back to North Platte to mop up puddles of chlorinated swimming water and then heading eight miles out of town to a dark and spooky cabin at three in the morning caused me to rethink some of my recent decisions.

One night about 2:30 A.M., after coming back from a game at Holdrege, I was squeegeeing the water off the locker room floor, barely awake, when I decided to play Fred Astaire. The plan was to put one hand on the countertop and smoothly vault over it without breaking stride or missing a beat. Singing "Born to Lose," I vaulted over the counter cleanly, but when my bare feet hit the wet floor, they shot forward with great speed and smashed into the lockers. I looked at my pained, throbbing right foot. Four smaller toes marched reasonably forward, but the big toe was doing a right oblique. It was surely broken, I thought.

I had the incessant rain to thank for giving the toe time to return to its normal color, size, and direction. I could not afford to go on the disabled list again after missing the first two weeks at McCook the year before with a cast on my foot. It wasn't good to get the reputation of having bad wheels when you depend on speed and quickness to hold a job. By the time the ballparks had dried out enough for us to play ball, I could run again. Counter-leaping would be left to Astaire until the season was over.

At the café I ordered a cup of coffee and dropped some coins into the jukebox. Kay Starr belted out "Bonaparte's Retreat" and "Side by Side," singing spirited, swinging harmony with herself on voice-over recordings. Things began to pick up. Maybe even "Blue Skies" tomorrow. We were due.

While we waited for the rain to let up enough to have a league game, we got together at Jeffers Field for practice one day when the mud wasn't too wet. A rugged right-handed pitcher, somewhat similar physically to muscular Bob Cerv though not quite as heavy, was taking some warmup tosses on the sideline. I remembered this pitcher well. One night the year before at McCook he had fired a curve ball to me which came at my head with such startling velocity that I flinched, lost my balance, and wound up on the ground. From that embarrassing location I heard Ed Manley call, "Strike!" The ball had broken so far and so fast it had caught the high-inside corner of the strike zone. At least Manley saw it that way (they did call a higher strike then). To say I felt foolish was an understatement. It was one of the hazards of always looking for a fast ball. It was also one of the protections.

This rough, hard-throwing right-hander had been known as "Fidgety Fred" Wells when he pitched two years before with the Lincoln A's. Always moving out there on the mound, impatiently waiting to rip the next pitch by the hitter, Fred presented an uneasy package to the new hitter, who sensed it might not be wise to dig in. Also, the stories went, he had trouble accepting criticism from the fans and would respond with salty words and gestures, which led to heated exchanges and even trips into the bleachers by Wells to resolve things physically. Freddy's terminal "rabbit-ears" made him a constant target of loudmouths, whom management had to forbid him to confront. It was that problem plus other constraints that had caused this free spirit to jump to semi-pro ball—much to the benefit of the receiving team.

At shortstop another muscular athlete smoothly positioned himself in front of a ground ball, came up, mechanically setting the ball by his ear, aimed over his extended glove hand, and fired the ball on a flat arc to first. Except when he had to hurry for the double play and would whip the ball from the ground, George Lebedz would always come up with the same set, fire, and watch another automatic putout. George had honed this seemingly measured and mechanical form to a highly dependable degree and was one of the surest-fielding, wide-ranging, and accurate-throwing shortstops in the game.

I didn't know how I would compare with Lebedz's second baseman of three years before. I wasn't even aware of a "Nellie Fox." While Fox was playing in Lincoln, I was in McCook, helping turn the Cats' baseball fortunes around, and Nellie hadn't yet played long enough to assemble his fine reputation. At the most, I knew vaguely that a second baseman from the Lincoln A's had made it to the majors, as had one of their pitchers, Bobby Shantz; a first baseman from the later Lincoln Chiefs, Dick "66 Home Runs" Stuart, would go up to the Pirates in 1958.

Joking around on the sidelines with happy, fifty-five-year-old Seth Negly, who was one of the most involved and supportive businessmen for the North Platte Plainsmen, was square-jawed, six-foot-one inch manager Bob Harris, now wearing brown horn-rimmed glasses—something he wouldn't have been caught dead in during his pitching days with the Detroit Tigers. Harris had pitched against the New York Yankees and won in 1938, when Joe DiMaggio had just come up. I later saw the box score. Bob just happened to have a well-worn copy in his wallet.

Harris crept over and goosed Negly with the knob end of a baseball bat, and Seth nearly jumped, cackling, over the fence. I concluded that Bob had a casual but firmly established relationship with management. After all, there weren't a whole lot of former major league pitchers—pitchers who had beaten the Yankees and could tell stories of fabled big league heroes—walking around loose in North Platte.

"DiMaggio was a hound," Harris said. "He was a real coxswain."

"You mean like Buzz?" I said.

"Well, I don't know if he could run with Powley," Harris said. "Joe was just a rookie then, you know."

"Come on, you guys," Buzz said. "I'm a married man now. Who started all these stories about me anyway?"

The talk about his glory days got Harris's adrenaline pumping, and he walked over to get his glove and a ball from the dugout. "Somebody warm me up," said the suddenly young forty-year-old manager. "Powley, grab that mitt," and he began lobbing the ball in a distinctive overhand motion, gradually stretching his once exceptional right arm. Soon the ball was coming right off Harris's ear and popping the mitt loudly. I walked over behind Powley to watch.

"You're throwing that ball pretty hard, Bob," I said. "Why don't you pitch for us some night?"

"Oh, no," Harris said, "I don't have it anymore. I used to be fast—real fast. I could really hum it!"

"Well," I said, "it still has a little hum on it."

"Yeah, but I could only go about an inning now, maybe two, and then they'd get to me good."

The longing look on Harris's face told me he really could once "hum" it with the best of them. And when he could, he stood tall—very tall. Making out the lineup card, coaching third base, and occasionally goosing middle-aged baseball groupies seemed to have made the Yankee killer a little shorter. And much older.

In the batter's box and cranking out long drives to and over the left-field fence was "King Kermit" Lewis, formerly with Superior and Holdrege, now playing first base for the Plainsmen. With Bill Denker playing third that year for North Platte (Lexington had had to drop out for a year and regroup financially), our infield looked as if it could hold its own with anybody. Even the Lincoln A's, since with Freddy Wells and George Lebedz we had about as many of the 1948 A's as the current Class A team did. It would be nice if the rain would stop so we could find out just how good we were.

The rain finally did stop. Brisk winds at last hurried the gray, broken clouds across the sky, allowing glimpses of almost forgotten blue to bring smiles to our overcast faces, and the 1951 NIL season resumed.

It was one of those mid-June mornings you hear so many Nebraskans talk about with great fondness. The sun was at last bright and warm. There was just a hint of a breeze. The sky was very blue with a few cottony cloud puffs lazily drifting over the sweet-smelling, rich-colored flowers and gently moving the tree leaves. The dreary, gray rain of so many recent days was forgotten, and only the vivid and welcome beauty of its product seemed to register on the faces of North Platte people.

I finished my breakfast of eggs over easy and coffee, dipping my last piece of whole wheat toast into the softness of the egg yolk, enjoying the delicious combination taste. There was no concern then for undercooked eggs. Salmonella was thought to be a new Superior infielder from New Jersey, not a health threat.

As I strolled down the sidewalk in the remarkable weather of this smiling morning, I became aware of a small gathering in front of Hinman's Motors. I counted manager Bob Harris, catcher Tom O'Connor, baseball groupie Seth Negly, and a few others I did not know. Harris and O'Connor had day jobs at Hinman's.

"What's going on, guys? Why aren't you inside selling cars?" I said.

"We're waiting for the parade," Harris said.

"What parade?" I asked.

"What parade!?" Harris said. "Don't you read the front pages of the paper, Hobe?"

"No, only the box scores on the sports page," I said. "And then only if I have a good game."

"It's the rodeo parade," Tom said.

"Oh, yeah," I remembered. "That is today, isn't it."

Dr. H. K. Young, the parade chairman, had announced that there were 130 entries, and that all participants were to gather "at the empty lot across from Snyder's Food Market between Dewey and Pine Streets." The parade would start promptly at 10:30 A.M.; it would "not wait for those not in place."

Pretty Lois Saeger, who was in charge of rodeo ticket sales, came up to us, wearing a light blue summer dress. She went right to Tommy O'Connor and stood close. They were, as we called it then, "going steady."

"How are tickets going, Lois?" Seth asked.

"Pretty good," she said, "but there are plenty of good seats left for all three performances."

Suddenly, from far down the street I heard the driving entrance notes to a jazz number so familiar to me it turned my head quickly. I listened intently to a few more bars of the distant call to action.

"That's Bix!" I said.

"What's Bix?" Harris said.

"That music," I said. As the sounds got closer, I could see a pickup truck with a speaker horn on the roof from which the clarion tones of Bix's cornet announced the opening ceremonies of the fifth annual Buffalo Bill Rodeo of North Platte.

What a way to start things off! I thought. Man, if "At the Jazz Band Ball" doesn't get you in the mood for a parade, you must be dead. Out there in the Sand Hills of Nebraska on this sleepy morning there was suddenly a feeling of Mardi Gras coming down the street. Who even had a Bix record out here in country-music central, I wondered? No speaker-blaring tones of sad Hank Williams or Eddie Arnold to lead this parade! This was no time for crying-in-your-beer music. This was call-to-rodeo-action time, and to my delight the parade's musical director had selected one of Beiderbecke's most spirited and famous jazz recordings to get things started.

I watched the speaker truck, enjoying every driving note, as it passed us and rolled slowly down the street. Behind it, the clicking and clopping of walking horses announced riders of all ages, attractively attired in Stetson hats and riding breeches and brightly colored silk neck scarves, all sitting comfortably erect and smiling at the people lining the street. Leading them once again was the popular "Buffalo Bill" Lee Case, in flowing beard and pioneer clothing.

Reigning as queen in 1951 was Gayle Gutherless of Brady. There were seven candidates for Junior Rodeo Queen, ranging from age ten to Marcia Deanne Shields, age four, riding "Trixie," a horse just thirty-nine inches tall. Open convertibles with pretty girls sitting on the top of the back seat and waving accented the specially designed floats with the rodeo theme and the novelty and specialty entries, four bands, and nine horse clubs that followed.

One of the passing riders caught the glance of all of us. "She sure looks good on a horse, doesn't she?" I said.

"She looks good in a bathing suit, too," Seth Negly said.

"How do you know?" Harris asked.

"She's a lifeguard at the swimming pool," Seth said. Harris gave him a suspicious look. "I like to go swimming," Seth added. Bob continued his look. "I'm a good swimmer—they do let us old guys in the pool too, you know," Seth concluded.

"Oh, sure," Harris said. "You just go there to look at Meise. You can't even dog-paddle."

"That's her name, 'Meise'?" I said.

"Her name is Mary Elise Day and she was last year's rodeo queen," Seth explained. "When she was a tiny girl she couldn't say her two names, and it came out, 'Meise.' That's what she's been called ever since."

"You sure do know a lot about her, Seth," Harris said.

"Well, I've lived here a long time," Negly said. "I know the family well."

"How well do you know this?" and Harris faked a "gotcha" grab. Seth jumped backward. Why, I thought, do I feel like I am in junior high gym class when I'm around these two guys?

One of the most popular features of the rodeo was the "Chuck Wagon Feed," sponsored again by St. Mary's Guild of the Episcopal Church of Our Savior, corner of Fourth and Vine. The "feed" was served in the church basement and offered a menu of prime ribs of beef, baked potatoes, tossed salad, cole slaw, Harvard beets, baked beans, garlic bread, homemade pie, coffee, and milk—all for $1.50 for adults, half price for children.

"Yellow Fever," a palomino owned by the Sandhill Rodeo Company of Gandy and North Platte, was a featured bucking bronco in the 1951 rodeo. This "seldom-ridden" horse had thrown eighteen of the last twenty cowboys who tried to ride him. And Yellow Fever was only one animal among the largest number of livestock entered to date in these annual rodeos.

The Buffalo Bill Rodeo was an enormous event in North Platte, not only involving a very large segment of the town's citizenry but captivating many small surrounding towns as well. Up-to-date results in all the roping and riding events were published daily on the front page of the *Telegraph-Bulletin*.

Even I had become involved that year, painting action figures of bucking broncos on storefront windows for ten dollars apiece. I used washable tempera, painting on the inside of the glass when I could, so that rain would not wash it away. Where I could only work outside, I coated the finished paintings with a clear varnish to waterproof them, and then scraped the windows clean with a razor blade after the rodeo. With the tempera between the varnish and the glass, the scraping was not as tedious as I first thought it might be.

During the weeks leading up to and through the performance days, the Buffalo Bill Rodeo rode tall in the saddle. Everything else in North Platte took a back seat. Even our powerful, league-leading semi-pro Plainsmen stepped back and enjoyed the excitement.

Max Quick

Sand Hills, Sunshine, and Hard Slides

When I was playing for the Cats, Leo McKillip was all-everything in high school sports in McCook. He excelled in football, basketball, track, baseball, and probably dodgeball in his early years. He was good enough in baseball to become a utility player for the McCook Cats.

McKillip was a catcher and an outfielder and I was a second baseman, so even though some town players may have regarded me as an intruder, I never thought I had personally taken anything away from him. We didn't have a lot to do with each other off the field in McCook, but I always assumed we were friends. And I still believe he was my friend—unlike Dollaghan and Haines, who occasionally threw at my head when I tried to hit.

Leo was good enough in football and track that Notre Dame recruited him, and he accepted, because the postwar 1940s were not counted among the great years of Nebraska football. He had a high hurdler's stride and covered the ground with a speed even greater than it appeared. At six-foot-three and about 190 pounds, McKillip at full speed was someone to avoid if possible.

That summer of 1951 when I joined North Platte, I found myself playing against Leo for the first time. He was a pretty good hitter and he reached first early in the game. I decided to cheat a little toward second so that I could be sure and get there in time to make the double play or stop him if he tried to steal.

Before he had a chance to try, the next hitter chopped a high bouncer to George Lebedz at short, and I raced over to cover, get the relay off, and get out of there fast. The ball seemed to take forever to reach George, but finally he fired it to me at second. I grabbed it, planting my left foot quickly to get something on the throw and then be ready to jump high over the sliding McKillip. As I took the ball from the glove to throw, I felt an explosion of pain about ten inches above the knee, and the ball and my body parts seemed to fly in all directions.

The pain high on my thigh was so strong I couldn't stay down on the ground. I had to get up to see if I still had a left leg. I limped around in circles, almost hopping because I could not put weight on my bruised thigh muscles and nearly fractured femur. I painfully called time, not even knowing what had happened to my aborted relay to first. I had been taken out by sliding runners at second many times on double plays, gone up and over their hard, rolling attempts to separate me from the ball, relaxing and riding with them, coming down sometimes with my feet higher than my head but usually with little pain. But this was the highest, hardest, and squarest hit I had ever taken from a flying knee at great speed, at the moment of the arrival of the ball. I could not be convinced at that moment that there wasn't some lingering hometown resentment toward imported college hotdogs who were brought in to replace the local town players. Bending over in pain, I turned to McKillip.

"Jeez, Leo!" I wheezed, "we're playing baseball here tonight. This isn't the 120-yard high hurdles!"

Leo didn't say anything. He was dusting himself off. As he bent to pick up his cap, I thought I saw him wince, and I was certain there was a bit of a limp as he jogged to the dugout. I hoped he had hurt his kneecap.

"Didn't you ever hear of sliding?" I called out in a painful parting shot. Leo had nothing to say and continued off the field. That's the trouble with playing all those sports so well and so hard. Sometimes it must be difficult to keep them all separate. I don't know how I did it, but thanks to the incredible will-to-play powers of youth, I managed to finish the game. I suppose I should have been thankful that one of Leo's events was not the long jump. At least I didn't get spiked.

Later that week I was at the café, having a cup of coffee and smoking a cigarette and feeling terrible. Why, I thought, did I ever get hooked on these damn cigarettes in Chicago? They burn my throat, I feel lousy after I've had one, but then in half an hour or sooner all I can think of is sucking in the smoke from another one to get my nicotine fix and burning my throat all over again. I had tried to quit but had been unable to do so. It would be many years—twelve to be exact—before I could.

Angelo Ossino walked into the café, and I waved him over.

"This coffee is lousy," I said. "You going to eat or just have coffee, Oz?"

"I was just going to have coffee."

"I feel like hell today. Let's go get a beer," I suggested. I was between jobs, and Oz didn't seem to be working either. So we left the little coffee shop to get a beer. I didn't usually drink anything in the afternoon at all, and not really much in the evening. But between the cigarette side effects, the bitter coffee, and a general depression about my immediate prospects off the ball field, I wanted a beer.

We sat at a bar sipping our brew, and I casually scanned the room for signs of anything interesting of the opposite sex. I was not much of an operator, and scanning was usually about all I did. The tavern was empty except for the bartender, two old guys down at the end of the bar, and one woman sitting alone in a booth sipping a drink. She was not particularly attractive; she had too much makeup on, was probably thirty or forty (which to me at that time was old), and just a little on the heavy side, so I brought my cool gaze back to the mirror behind the bartender—and caught a glimpse of my own face. My God, I thought, I look grim! We drank in silence for a minute or two. Angelo—a stocky, medium-tall, thirty-year-old bachelor who had been a standout curve ball pitcher in American Legion baseball in Omaha and could still break off a good curve ball, if not overpower anybody with his fast ball—took his turn scanning the sparsely populated interior of this town saloon.

"See that woman sitting alone over there?" Oz said, returning to his beer.

"Yeah," I said. "I don't need to ask which one, because I know she's the only one in here."

"She's been giving you the eye," Oz said. I casually scanned again, nonchalantly checking her out, and then returned to the mirror.

"What do you mean, giving me the eye?" I said. "You only looked over there for two seconds."

"I can tell," Oz said.

"How do you know she isn't giving you the eye?" I said.

"No, she's looking at you. Why don't you smile at her? Don't look so serious." I looked at my face in the mirror again. I didn't look just serious; I looked downright unfriendly. I took another swallow of beer. Hell, lighten up, I thought. Is this the way I look all the time? The very possibility depressed me even more. I asked for another beer.

"Why don't you go over and talk to her?" Angelo said. "I just saw her smile at you.

"If you saw her smile," I said, "then she was smiling at you. She's not smiling at the back of my head."

"Hobe, give her a smile before you scare her away," Oz said.

"You give her a smile," I said. "You go talk to her. I don't think she's my type." I began to think Oz really wanted to meet her but was too shy to go over and start a conversation. He wasn't still a bachelor at thirty because he had great self-confidence with women. I was sure he wanted me to break the ice. Angelo didn't know I was a slow operator too. Besides, I really wasn't attracted to this woman, who looked a little sad and uninteresting.

"You're sure a lot of fun today," Oz said. "I should have had a cup of coffee." We drank in silence for a little while.

"Sorry," I said. "I guess I'm just having a bad day." I reached for a cigarette, glared at it, but lit it anyway. I drew in some smoke. The first two or three puffs were the only ones that didn't burn my throat. My body is trying to tell me something, I thought. It's saying this lousy smoke doesn't belong inside my throat and lungs! Angelo and I drank quietly some more. "Seriously, Oz," I said, "why don't you go over and talk to her? You look a hell of a lot friendlier than I do. Just look at us in the mirror. If I had to go out with one of us, I would choose you." I ground the cigarette out in the ashtray, less than half smoked. Oz looked over his shoulder to reconsider.

"She's gone now, anyway," he said. We drank our beer and thought about the next game. Or the last game. The bartender asked if we wanted another beer, but we waved him off. "I've got to be going," Oz said.

"Yeah," I said, "me too."

We really didn't have to be going. We didn't have anywhere to go. But wherever it was we were going, we felt it would have to top where we were just then.

Johnny Mathis, our right fielder and pitcher, had a pretty sister named Dorothy who was married to manager Bob Harris. The Harrises had a house with a homemade beauty parlor in the back section, where Dot worked as hair stylist and beauty operator for the North Platte ladies. I had tired of living in a bedroom I'd rented in a family home when I left my cabin, and I'd mentioned that I wanted to move to something more like an apartment. So when Bob and Dot decided to move the beauty equipment into another room and turn the shop into a nice little apartment with a refrigerator and a private side door, I was happy to rent it. I could have dry cereal and milk for breakfast and sandwiches and milk for lunch; when I wanted to eat out big, I could go to a café and dine on chicken-fried steak and apple pie a la mode to the background musical strains of Ernest Tubb and Roy Acuff. And, of course, keep a few cold bottles of Schlitz or Pabst Blue Ribbon on the refrigerator shelves.

One evening I was listening to Bix driving through his great solo on "Sorry" on my small record player in my new apartment. While I really did identify—and even find solace—with Eddie Arnold, Hank Williams, and Roy Acuff and their songs of perpetual rejection and loneliness, the bad hand fate had always dealt them, and the eternal emptiness of their mailboxes, I found it necessary to play something a little more upbeat now and then in order to keep going.

I was in the middle of admiring the timeless clarity of Bix's unique attack on his cornet solo when I heard a knock at my door. I opened it and saw Ronnie Bennett, our muscular (muscle-bound by the baseball standards of 1952) third baseman; he had been re-cruited all the way from Stillwater, Oklahoma, where he starred as halfback on the Oklahoma State Cowboys football team.

"Hobe," Ronnie said, almost whispering, "what are you doing right now?"

"Not much," I said, looking around outside, as if I expected to find something. "Why?"

"I need you to help me out. Come on out to the car."

"What for?" I said.

"I need some time," Ronnie said. "Just come out to the car with me."

"Time for what?" I said.

"I've got 'M' out in the car. We had some beers, and then I got in the back seat with her," Ron said. "She wants to go again, right now. I can't just yet. I need a little time. She's like all over me."

"Well, jeez, Ron," I said, "you're too fast. You have to take a little more time with a woman."

"Come on, Hobe," Ron said. "She wants you while I recuperate. She said so. It was her idea to come over here and get you."

"Look, Ron," I said. "'M' is not half bad, but she is married. Her husband is working the evening shift right downtown. Maybe that doesn't bother you, but that would worry me a little."

"Oh, hell," Ronnie said. "He doesn't care!"

"You mean, she doesn't care," I said. "You don't know about him." Ronnie looked around nervously and with a little exasperation. Our voices were getting louder.

"Oh, just come on out to the car and talk to her, Hobe," Ron said. "Just give me fifteen or twenty minutes and I'll be ready to go again."

"I don't think so," I said. "I don't want her husband coming after me."

"He doesn't know what's going on and doesn't care, I'm telling you," Ron said. "He couldn't whip you anyway."

"Well," I said, "I'm thinking more like coming after me with a gun."

"Oh shit, Hobe," Ron said, "you worry about things more than anybody I've ever known!"

"Yeah, I'm crazy that way. I worry about husbands who think I'm humping their wives."

"Come on, Hobe. Just come out to the car and we'll drive around for a little while. You don't even have to do anything," Ron said.

"It sounds like I won't have to," I said. "It sounds like she'll be all over me before I get the car door shut."

"Are you going with me or not?" Ron said.

"No, Ron," I said, "I don't think so. You know I'd like to help you out, but I don't like the possible side effects here."

"Well, what am I going to tell her?" Ron said.

"Tell her I have the stomach flu."

Bennett gave me one last pleading look, which I rejected, and then he walked down the little sidewalk to his car. After a few minutes the car started up and moved slowly down the street.

Another difficult decision had been made in the life of a horny, single, semi-pro second baseman, guided by a long-standing fear of and respect for possible unpleasant consequences.

Johnny Rego and I were very good friends when we played at the University of Nebraska. Johnny was a good little hustling, all-round shortstop from New Jersey, but he'd had the same timing misfortune during part of his college tenure as my brother Don: they came along at the same time as Bob Grogan and Bill Denker. Grogan, as noted before, was an outstanding shortstop who could hit the long ball. As long as he was around, nobody could move the Spider out of the lineup. My brother, a very good third baseman, would have had to beat out the best third baseman in the Big Seven, Bill Denker, to get any time playing third, or beat out me at second, which he could also play very well. He did get some college time in the outfield.

In the NIL, Johnny Rego started playing at Lexington with Bill Denker, but in 1951, when Lexington had to take the year off and Bill played for North Platte, he played for McCook.

During one important game at Jeffers Field in North Platte, Rego hit a sharp ground ball right back through the mound. I broke for the ball, and though I had a great jump, I thought, no way can I get this one. But I went on hard to try and backhand it. I was hot because I had just made an error, and the adrenaline must have been flowing. I still don't know how, but as I reached for it on the dead run, the ball came up and stuck in the tip of the web of my glove. Well, I thought, this is really something. Now let's see if I can get some kind of a throw off to first and make it close. From far behind second I turned and fired the ball in the direction of Kermit Lewis at first, and then I fell down. I didn't see the throw clearly, but the crowd roar told me it had beat Johnny to the base and was on target.

What happened then came as a jarring surprise. Rego, bouncing wildly about, threw his cap down and stomped on it, briefly reminding me of Yosemite Sam in a Bugs Bunny cartoon. "What the hell are you doing!?" he screamed. "You never made a play like that in your life!!"

He was right. I hadn't thought I would even touch it.

"I needed that hit!" he continued. "What's the matter with you? That was a base hit! That ball should have gone through!"

Suddenly feeling terrible, I almost went over and apologized to Yosemite John. The ball should have gone through, and almost any other day of my life it would have. Or at least my wild throw would have pulled Kermit off the bag. It wasn't fair, I thought—a play like that, maybe my best ever through the middle, and the out had to happen to a good friend. I guess Tony Sharpe was right. When I get mad I sometimes become a fielding fool and don't even know my own limitations. But why couldn't that ball have been hit by Art Dollaghan or some guy lower on my list of favorite players? It just wasn't right that I should feel like a criminal. I should have been able to enjoy this play more. I was sorry that John was in a slump and that I prolonged it.

I didn't know. It's lonely at the top.

By contrast, a game at Fairgrounds Park in McCook a few weeks after the Cats' management had let me go without advance notice made me feel all warm inside. Mickey Stubblefield tried to go up the ladder on me, and I took him deep off the top of the scoreboard in center field at the 400-foot marker for a triple.

Mickey's fast ball that night was very fast, so I guess that's why he stayed with it. When will they learn, I wondered, you don't get me out with the fast ball? Mick almost had me, but after two or three foul balls straight back, I hit the highest, longest ball of my NIL life. It would have been out if it hadn't been so high; in fact, I was surprised Eddie Miller hadn't caught it. It must have come down too high up on the scoreboard for him to reach it.

As we passed between innings—I'd been stranded at third—Eddie Miller grinned and said, "Where'd you get all that power?!" My grin was wider than Eddie's for the first time since we'd met. For a few minutes I felt some of the old glow for the game again.

The yo-yo of emotions a ballplayer may experience even during a single play was sharply evident in a game where I hit another triple. Our infield was still muddy, and most of my attention was on cleaning my spikes. Then I pounded a ball off the right-center-field fence. Rounding first, I felt as if I were running on two half-dried mud pies. I chugged for second, gathering more mud by the step, and prepared to slide—or flop—into second for a double. But the outfielders were having a little trouble picking up the ball, and Bob Harris, manager and third-base coach, waved me on. I took the turn and seemed to be nearly in left field, skidding and releasing chunks of mud in all directions. To my great surprise, Harris held his hands high for me to stand up. They must really be slipping and falling over each other out there, I thought.

Gasping for air with my hands on my knees, I marveled at my reaching third safely after what seemed like a very long and tedious journey through the mud. Harris put his hand on my shoulder and looked into my face to be sure I was listening.

"Nobody out!" he said. "Make the ball be through. Don't get caught off!" I nodded. I couldn't have talked if I'd wanted to. "Nobody out!" he repeated. "Watch out for line drives!" I nodded a little stronger, as if to say, I know how to run bases.

I began to take a short lead, my eyes fixed on the pitcher's stretch. My breath was coming back, and I was starting to enjoy the accomplishment of the triple. The pitcher delivered. Whack! George Lebedz pulled a curve ball hard down the line. The drive caught me with my weight slightly to my right side. I turned back to the bag with the crossover step as the third baseman made a back-handed stab at the one-hopper and, with his momentum, stood between me and third base. I stopped abruptly, rolling my ankle slightly on the ball of mud under my left shoe, and did some rapid assessment of the situation. Number one, I was dead. I had been caught leaning. If I wanted to stay away from a double play, I had to get into a rundown to give Lebedz time to get to first. That meant reversing my direction as quickly as possible because the third baseman was now coming to tag me and send the ball on to first for two. I turned and did my best Richie Ashburn imitation long enough for George to get to first before they tagged me.

Having not fully gotten my breath after the triple, I bent over again, sucking in the damp night air and peeking at Bob Harris. He was standing in the coaching box, hands on hips and his back to me, staring motionless far out over the left-field fence in foul territory. There was only one thing to do. Go to the bench and sit down.

We were all feeling great in North Platte in late August 1952. Two years in a row we had won the NIL championship and were now readying ourselves for the second important part of the season—the Shaughnessy playoffs. Our forty-one-year-old manager, former Detroit Tiger pitcher Bob Harris, had guided the strong Plainsmen through a second impressive summer. Pitchers Fred Wells, Clyde Anderson, and John Mathis were well rested and in good health. Our infield, leading the league in double plays, was sound and performing at peak level, and our hard-hitting outfield couldn't be better. We were ready.

It was in the middle of the night and I was asleep when the phone rang in my small apartment.

"Hello," I said.

"Hobe—?" The voice on the other end of the line sounded far away.

"Yes?"

"This is Fred—Fred Wells—"

"Fred!" I said. "What's up?" There was a long pause.

"—I've had an accident," Wells said.

"Are you hurt?! Where are you?"

"I don't know—some farmhouse south of town."

"Are you hurt? Should I call an ambulance?"

"Hobe—I'm in trouble," he said. "I fucked up."

"What do you mean?"

"I hurt my shoulder when I smashed up my car."

"Which shoulder?" I demanded. "Your pitching one?"

"Yeah—" Fred said.

"How bad is it?"

"I can't even lift my arm," Fred said, almost crying. "I think I tore something loose. I think it's really fucked up."

"Do you need me to take you to the hospital?" I said.

"No—I—the people here are going to call the police. They say they think I need medical attention."

I still couldn't make things fit. There was something missing in this conversation. Why was I the one talking to Fred in this situation?

"Fred," I asked, "are you sure you don't want me to come get you? Why did you call me?"

"I crashed the car out near your cabin, I think," Fred said. "I thought you might be able to come get me and I could stay there overnight, or at least until I got myself together. I can't go back to town just yet—I wasn't thinking—I've had a few beers. I know it's a dumb idea now."

"I don't live there anymore, Fred. I moved into town some time ago. How did you get this number?" I said.

"I asked the operator."

"Do you want me to call Bob Harris?"

"No, no—not yet! He'll really be pissed! I've got to think. Let me think some things out."

I tried to clear my own head of sleep. The ringing phone had shaken me up. I thought I heard Fred crying on the other end of the line.

"Are you okay, Fred?" I asked. "Let me talk to those people there, Fred."

"Yeah," he said, "I'm okay now. I just let everybody down. I'm through for the year. Shit, I can't even lift my arm."

"Did you call your wife yet? Do you want me to call her?"

"No! Don't call her yet! I've got to think this through—"

I thought some more. Time seemed to drift by so slowly just then. I didn't know where to go from there. Fred had never really talked much to me before, so I was surprised he had called me. But since he had, I felt I had to think clearly because I knew that Fred, with a six-pack of Schlitz in him, could not.

"We were going so good—we were going to win it all again," Fred muttered.

I tried to think of something to pick up his spirits. He sounded near tears again.

"Hell, Fred," I said. "We'll win it anyway. Sure, we'll miss your pitching, but we'll just have to suck it up and play harder. Why don't you call Harris as soon as the police get there and tell him where you are? I think he would want to know. Hell, I *know* he would. After all, Fred, you've been our big gun all year. You got us here—"

"Oh, yeah, well, and Clyde got us here too. Without Anderson, I wouldn't have been enough. And Johnny too—"

"It's going to be okay," I said. "You just get that shoulder fixed up."

"They want me to get off the phone now," Fred said. "They want to call the police."

I thought it was ironic that Johnny Mathis was also a cop. "Maybe Johnny will be on duty tonight," I said.

"Yeah," Fred said, trying to laugh. "He'll kick my ass for hurting my arm. Sorry I bothered you, Hobe. I wasn't thinking too good after the crash. I thought you were still out there in that cabin. I think I hit my head on something, too. I've got to go now. I don't feel so good."

"You take care of yourself," I said as I heard him hang up the phone.

The sports page of the *Telegraph-Bulletin* for September 2, 1952, reported that North Platte, behind the solid pitching of Bill Best, late-season addition to the pitching staff, had evened up the series of the first round of the playoffs against the Superior Knights. Next to the account of the game was this three-paragraph announcement:

Chances of North Platte winning the Shaughnessy baseball playoff of the Nebraska Independent League took a jolt Monday night when Fred Wells, ace pitcher, suffered an injury in an automobile accident.

Ligaments were torn loose in his right shoulder and he will be out of action for at least two weeks, which for all practical purposes, means the remainder of the season.

Manager Bob Harris may be able to bring in Max Quick, of Stromsburg, however. Quick is eligible to pitch for the Plainsmen.

Nevertheless, without Fred Wells, North Platte did not win the Shaughnessy playoffs that year. Fred knew, and the rest of us knew, that his loss was too much for the team to overcome.

Floyd Stickney

Roaring to Bankruptcy

By 1952 the rumblings of NIL fiscal indigestion, barely audible during 1948, were so loud that everyone in the league had to pay attention. Following that first year, when McCook began to gobble up outside players, the NIL took a financial roller-coaster ride that would upset the stomachs of many riders, creating an unhealthy degree of anxiety and animosity that threatened the league's success and even its continued existence.

The popular image of the "semi-pro" ballplayer was that of someone who played for money, yes, but not much money (he needed a day job too), whereas the professional, signed by a major or minor league team, played for enough more money to make a living from baseball. In 1946 in the NIL this was reasonably accurate. McCook's players, for example, nearly all of whom were local town athletes then, received a mere $2.50 to $3.00 a game. By 1955, just nine years later, salaries had soared to as high as $750 per month for pitchers, and other players averaged $350, according to McCook center fielder Eddie Miller, who rode out the NIL's eight-year existence.

Thus, what separated pro and semi-pro in the 1950s became less the amount of money than the degree of ownership. A semi-pro was only "semi-owned" by the management of the team he played for. He could do about anything with his life he wanted to as long as he showed up sober for games and produced. Contrast that to the life of "organized" ball players: minor league professionals lived on tight meal money and adhered to strict travel schedules, curfews, and other rules laid down by management.

And as for money, the semi-pro player of the late 1940s through the mid-1950s made more from his baseball job *plus* whatever day jobs (usually not extremely taxing) he chose than most minor league players. Some even made more than marginal players in the majors. A top pitcher in the NIL at this time, for example, could pitch once or twice a week for $100 to $150 a game and be a wheat farmer, a grocery store owner, a liquor store clerk, or a car salesman during the day. He would have more to spend than many minor league pitchers, in addition to more freedom and control of his life.

A good infielder or hard-hitting outfielder in 1948 could make anywhere from $150 to $300 a month playing baseball, depending on his résumé, and work during the day at a variety of jobs. A college hotdog would naturally not pick up as big a check as a former Triple-A Pacific Coast slugger or a veteran who'd led the league in hitting for Memphis in the Southern Association. But by 1956 non-pitchers were averaging $350 a month for baseball playing alone and operating in the mode of free agency.

Walt Charlesworth, who was a catcher for Holdrege and wrote a sports column for the *Holdrege Citizen*, released the information from one of his reliable sources that McCook businessmen were called upon to "fork over" hundreds of dollars above and beyond the gate receipts in order to meet the monthly payroll of the high-flying 1948 Cats. From what I knew, this was probably true. In fact, in a feature about the NIL that appeared in the 1982 *McCook Gazette* centennial issue, Eddie Miller revealed that one year the McCook Baseball Board raised $40,000 but still lost money.

From the *Kearney Hub* sports page of June 11, 1948, came this comment: "Looking over the McCook lineup, it is easy to see that the citizens of the southwestern city are eager to win ball games— or buy them, as the case may be." And the case was that after 1948 everybody in the NIL was out to "buy them." Previously, most of the money had been concentrated on pitching. Now, every position was being examined from both the offensive and the defensive point of view. So determined were the Superior Knights to catch up with the freewheeling NIL that in the early 1950s they advertised in the *Sporting News* for pro ballplayers from Class B or higher. When Barc Wade of the *Kearney Hub* conducted a write-in vote for an all-star team at the end of 1948—just the first year of serious NIL outside recruitment—seven of the selections on the starting nine were players from outside the league area.

McCook led off with its three-infielder contingent from the 1948 University of Nebraska Big Seven champions—the beginning of a long roster of Huskers in NIL teams such as Lexington and North Platte. Holdrege had its potent Denver connection in 1949, and Superior its pipeline from the Waterloo, Iowa, Class B Three-I League in 1950; these sources produced a profound improvement on each team. North Platte imported a stellar group from Lincoln (Class A Western League) and Canada as well as Nebraska U. The whole NIL was becoming stocked with professional veterans.

With Lexington sitting out the 1951 season, Lefty Haines was quickly signed by the highest bidder, the Kearney Irishmen. As Howard Baxter, sports scribe for the *Kearney Hub*, wrote on May 1, 1951, "Lefty was throwing 'twisters' before a number of the lads who saw action Sunday saw the light of day for the first time. Mr. Haines represents the major investment in the Kearney baseball association's salary scale. The old timer's years perhaps make that investment a bit of a gamble but there was little to indicate Sunday that he won't be as important to the Irish cause as any other single member of Mike Hollinger's squad."

Lefty was very proud of his reputation and the big money he was paid because of it. That same summer, while playing for North Platte, I lined a very hard single off his tough curve, and he knocked me down with the first pitch my next time up, just to remind me of who he was. Since I did not have a track record of hitting him, he wanted me to think twice about starting one.

The NIL had been getting so good that in 1952 Jimmy Kirkman in his North Platte sports column began urging a playoff system between the NIL and the other top semi-pro league in Nebraska, the Pioneer Nite League. Kirkman wanted a champion crowned between the leagues right then, since North Platte was playing at its absolute peak on its way to a second straight NIL title. So strong were the Plainsmen in 1951 and 1952 that manager Bob Harris wrote in 1952 to Denver, Colorado Springs, Pueblo, Lincoln, and Omaha of the Class A Western League, trying to book exhibition games. All those teams declined the invitation, despite guaranteed gate receipts. They said it was because of scheduling difficulties, but some of us suspected that it was also because it would not look good to get knocked off by a semi-pro team out in the Nebraska Sand Hills—which could very likely have happened. After all, Freddy Wells had been doing just that to Class A teams regularly when he pitched for the Lincoln A's two years before.

But just as the idea of a national college football playoff constantly meets with obstacles, the NIL had trouble putting into action either a semi-pro interleague championship series or exhibitions with teams in the Western League. Everyone agreed that both ideas would draw great crowds and help pull the NIL out of the financial quicksand. But end-of-season problems—such as some players having to report back to fall college student, coaching, teaching, and even administrative positions—made the late September timing of such games too great of an obstacle to overcome. It was difficult enough to hold the teams together through the Shaughnessy playoffs. A few exhibition games between the NIL and the Pioneer Nite League proved highly competitive and promising, but that's as far as the idea was able to go.

The possible destruction of the NIL from runaway salaries was brought early and strongly into print by Bill Madden, sportswriter for the *Hastings Tribune*. Bill had witnessed the effects of trying to keep up with the escalating salaries of expensive players: after winning the 1947 NIL title, Hastings couldn't raise enough player money to be a competitor in 1948. It did collect enough to make it back into the league in 1949, but by July 15 Bill was warning that "unless financial contributions are forthcoming immediately, the Hastings Sultans will not be able to finish the NIL baseball season." This was a stern wake-up call to the businessmen of Hastings who were not fulfilling their pledges. Madden continued, "Hastings is the largest city in the NIL and draws business from all member towns and this baseball is one of the best promoters of inter-city relations we have." But, the concerned sports scribe repeated, "the Sultans will have to have financial support right now and of sufficient amount, or the Hastings Baseball Association will be forced to drop the team from the NIL."

Three days later Madden broadened his perspective: "There's talk making the rounds that Hastings isn't the only NIL entry which is having trouble keeping afloat." And two days after that he again discussed his understanding of the league's fiscal woes: "The grapevine has it that there will be a meeting soon to decide what is to be done about some of the loop's high salaried players who are about to run their respective teams into a financial hole."

Hastings, after Madden's constant and shrill warnings, did manage to raise enough money to finish the 1949 season, but Bill, unhappy with his Sultans' poor showing against their higher-paid and more skilled NIL opponents, passed on the following gloomy advice on to his readers: "The situation which occurred this year was similar to the one in 1947 [bankrupting levels of overspending, apparently], only worse . . . and if the Hastings Baseball Association is smart it will see to it that it does not occur again." Hastings did see to it that it would not occur again. It dropped out of the NIL in 1950 and failed to rally enough financial support to return before the league folded.

The delicate chemistry demanded to sustain an expensive semi-pro team seemed to depend not only on baseball interest but on town size. The smaller towns focused with more collective dedication on a "town team" than did the larger towns, which had to spread civic wealth among more diversified interests and activities.

On July 27, 1949, Hastings "town crier" Bill Madden again tried to focus the public's attention on why he thought the NIL was floundering and doomed. "It is common talk," Madden wrote, "that more than one NIL entry has had or is having trouble meeting financial obligations. . . . The league constitution is again to blame. . . . Rule nine says in part, there is no salary limit and players may be drawn from anywhere. In other words, any NIL team, if it had the money, could hire a top notch major leaguer, provided of course he wanted to accept the offer."

I don't believe that Mr. Madden on his gloomiest Monday could have imagined what actually took place in McCook on May 30, 1954. The *McCook Gazette* headlines trumpeted, "Martin, Three Others to Play." This Billy Martin was of the New York Yankees, fresh from having the World Series of any ballplayer's life: breaking Babe Ruth's record of nineteen total bases in seven games, and tying the record for most base hits with twelve.

Billy was doing some military time at Fort Carson, Colorado, and playing on its baseball team, where McCook manager Tom Sutak first saw pitcher Ted Monroe. After watching Monroe strike out twenty-one Goodland, Kansas, hitters, Sutak had gone to get him to pitch for McCook. When Tom learned that some big leaguers—Billy Martin; Don Davis, a hard-hitting shortstop under contract with the Yankees; and Len Vandehy, New York Giants' property—were also in camp, he worked up a package deal that not only brought a record-breaking crowd to the McCook ballpark, but probably put the Baseball Board dangerously in debt.

It also caused some controversy. Printed reactions appeared as far away as the *Chicago Tribune*. One man in Iowa wanted to know why "Private Martin" was issued a pass on Saturday to play a semipro game with McCook against Kearney in Nebraska, while his infantry regiment was packing to move to a training camp on Tuesday.

This big league contingent from Fort Carson reportedly did cost an enormous price, but some would figure it was worth it, since the four contributed nine of thirteen runs and eleven of thirteen hits to McCook's 13-to-8 win. It might be noted, though, that Kearney batters raised a few eyebrows with their performance against Monroe's pitching, roughing him up for eight runs and fourteen hits. The Irishmen had been NIL champs the year before.

As for Billy Martin, he did not disappoint the overflowing crowd; his 3 for 4 included a home run and a double, and he fielded flawlessly, despite—as brother Don wrote to me—having an extremely sore arm. Don was the one bumped from his position to make room for Billy and had mixed feelings about the adjustment.

Although Bill Madden sourly blamed the NIL constitution for the runaway salary situation, its rival Pioneer Nite League's regulations were nearly as favorable for managers. In 1951 the PNL Board of Directors ruled that each team could have seven players from outside its territory and play as many as six in the lineup at the same time—almost the same player balance as the NIL teams had. So it would appear that the NIL constitution was not as irresponsible as Madden charged. Nevertheless, he summed up the frustration and sour grapes of the teams being left in the dust that year by asserting, "Most of towns in the league have gone overboard to get the best paid players they can, fellows who have no interest in the respective towns other than the paycheck. . . . The hometown boys as a whole are completely ignored."

As to hometown boys being ignored, I don't think Mr. Madden fully understood just what was happening. If a hometown lad could throw a fast ball eighty-eight or ninety miles an hour and find the plate with regularity, and if he had a sharp-breaking curve ball, he would get plenty of attention from the baseball boards. Or, if the local favorite son was very fast afoot, could hit .280 or better against pitching of the Dave Garland, Lefty Haines, Walt Ibsen quality, and could make the defensive plays in the clutches, he would be right in the lineup. After all, the expense of his room and board would already be taken care of, and he would probably start at rookie wages.

Bobby Reynolds, a star high school and university athlete, was a perfect example. Bob played for Nebraska as a standout second baseman and great football running back. His hometown was Grand Island, and when it joined the NIL, he was hired to play for its team because he could hit, field, and steal bases at a level necessary to exist in the league. And before Reynolds there were, among others, Eddie Miller and Gene Dellenbach of McCook, Irv Coufal and Lefty Haines of Lexington, Del Harris and Gerald Peterson of Kearney, and Paul Ward and Johnny Mathis of North Platte—all of them hometown players who remained throughout the expensive upgrading of the NIL because they were good enough to compete.

No, if the hometown lads were "being ignored," it was because they couldn't make the grade in a tough league that was bringing in better and better players by the year, many with professional experience. And to keep a team competitive—to make the top four in the year-end standings and thus qualify for the Shaughnessy playoffs, thereby securing enough money for the following year's salaries—required that inferior hometown players had to be passed over for superior imported players.

The question was asked, "How does the NIL compare with the Class A Western League?" One veteran McCook fan, who had seen many Lincoln Athletics games as well as NIL games, said, "The hitting and fielding are about the same, but the pitching in the NIL is considerably better." Barc Wade reported in 1948 in his *Kearney Hub* sports column that former major leaguer Mort Cooper, who'd been released from the Giants in 1947, was interested in pitching for Superior in 1949. One wise guy wasn't far off when he cracked, "It's a good thing he wanted to pitch for Superior. He couldn't break into the rotation at McCook or Holdrege."

In June 1952 Hank Williams was brought to Superior to pitch a game against North Platte, which later that year won its second consecutive NIL title. Williams had pitched 15 and 10 for Denver of the Class A Western League the year before, but North Platte won that contest 14 to 9, knocking Williams out of the game early.

The NIL pitching was enriched by many years of high-level baseball experience, talent, athletic ability, and (probably as important as anything) longevity. I don't know what they did differently then, but those old semi-pros kept their arms live far longer than they seem to be doing today, and some of them would pitch as often as every three or four days during the summer, sometimes even hiring out to other teams in the days between.

The following list of quality NIL moundsmen, almost all of whom I hit against, could make up the starting rotation for nearly a dozen formidable teams: Walt Ibsen, "Lefty" Haines, Bill Gardner, Dave Garland, Fred Wells, Paul Hiller, Ed McCarthy, Frank Sajavec, Ben Drieth, Mel Nicolai, Ed Van Nordheim, Roman Roh, Mickey Stubblefield, Clyde Anderson, Chuck Eisenmen, Art Dollaghan, Al Thune, Max Quick, Angelo Ossino, Tom Hurd, Bill Best, Jim McMahon, Johnny Mathis, Ray Novak, Chuck Wright, George Dockins, Ralph Germano, Marvin Dreffs, "Babe" Fidler, Bob Swanson, Jake Bornschlegel, Leon Foulk, "Lefty" Mazell, John Willingham, Marion Moss, Lowell Grosskoft, Tom Brookshire, and Caroll Beringer.

It was common knowledge out in southwestern Nebraska that if you couldn't really pitch, you didn't last long in an NIL game. What happened to Joe Paniak, Class B hurler jobbed in to pitch for Superior in 1949, was not uncommon. McCook batted around on him in the first inning and sent him to the bench in shock early. Many pitchers took up the challenge of pitching in the league, and to be asked back a second time was a high accomplishment.

After legendary pioneer Walt Ibsen, "Lefty" Haines comes to mind as NIL veteran poster boy. Haines was not just one of the best pitchers ever to stay home on the farm but a complete ballplayer. He could play first or outfield when he was younger and not pitching, and was still a dangerous hitter at nearly forty years of age. In those days, and especially in the NIL, pitchers could all hit. They not only could but liked to hit. Art Dollaghan would bat cleanup or fifth, whether he was pitching or playing outfield or first. Max Quick would also bat cleanup and was hired purely for his hitting between his pitching starts. They could all be counted on to help themselves win games at the plate. There was no such thing as a "wasted" at-bat.

In July 1953 our North Platte manager, Bob Harris, and Johnny Mathis, who had replaced Kermit Lewis as first baseman, had to be out of town on business during a game with McCook. Since we didn't have anyone else who had played much first base, a one-game substitute was needed. And since by 1953 the NIL was playing "Can You Top This?" in player salaries, the Plainsmen decided to go all out on this one.

Over in Hastings, Johnny Hopp was playing golf and relaxing at his driving range in his first year away from the major leagues. Three years before, as a utility player with 345 times at the plate, he had been just seven percentage points behind National League batting champ Stan Musial, and just one year earlier he had played briefly with the New York Yankees. The North Platte management decided he would do, so they signed Johnny Hopp to replace Johnny Mathis for one game.

Granted, Hopp was a little rusty, since this was his first game of the season. But he managed just one hit, a double, in five at-bats, and McCook pitcher John Willingham struck him out three times.

The Party's Over

For six years I returned to those little towns of southwest Nebraska for summers of adventure while working at my favorite job, baseball. Yet with each year came a measure of increased uneasiness. In my rookie season at McCook, when I looked at Kermit Lewis playing first base at thirty-eight years of age and in great athletic shape, I thought, I can do this until I'm thirty-eight. But at twenty-seven, with hardly any special anticipation left for the game though actually playing as well as ever, I concluded that doing this until I was thirty-eight was completely out of the question, and it had nothing to do with staying in physical shape.

While I was still in college, it was easy to be in shape for the NIL season, coming right off the competitive field of conference and interconference battles. Our hitting eyes were sharp, and we were finely tuned and in near midseason form. But after graduation from the University of Nebraska, I began a few seasons without that built-in spring training. Attendance at the Chicago Art Institute, teaching at Kansas State University, and working on my Master of Fine Arts degree at Wichita University meant that I faced my last three years with the problem of catching up with the NIL gang—which, as documented, was tougher each time I arrived. I had not looked at any pitching, even in batting practice, or done much running. When I look back, I am very impressed with my ability to jump in and play ball that well, that much out of tune. But I did, somehow, and at the time thought nothing of it. My performance continued at the high level necessary to remain in an NIL lineup,

Walt Ibsen

and each year my ignorance of Ted Williams's theory of just how difficult it is to hit a fast-traveling round object with a round piece of wood allowed me to step in and play as if I hadn't even been away. In fact, at age twenty-seven in 1953—my last year in the NIL—I believe I was playing the best ball of my life.

But the "baseball bum" specter, which I had once regarded with humor and pity, was now uncomfortably near. I could hear its labored breathing behind me. I envisioned myself years in the future, standing around the showroom at Hinman's Motors in North Platte and watching Bob Harris, now wearing a hearing aid, hobble over to goose a cackling Seth Negly with his cane, and Seth nearly jumping out of his walker. And I saw myself sitting with a cup of black coffee, and noticeably thinning hair, in the small café talking to some red-faced rookie about the women I never found in North Platte or McCook, while Hank Williams's backwoods tones informed us "No Letter Today," and Eddie Arnold again notified me that he was "Born to Lose."

What was the "baseball bum" story? What was the source of that denigrating label stuck on many of my older associates? Was this leering, grizzled specter ready to take me to the "land of Bumdom" with sore arm and tired knees? Lurking as part of my possible future, it forced me to make some life choices sooner than I had expected.

The profile of this creature began usually with a boy signing a major league contract shortly after or before high school graduation, being sent to Class D ball, working his way up the system until it was determined he had reached his peak, and then being cut and sent out into the world to support himself, like an ex-con paroled from prison. Such a lad, now a diamond-weary veteran, having never gone to college or even technical school, drifted from place to place doing what he had been trained to do—playing baseball. When his body broke down, or the small-town baseball teams that would still hire him went bankrupt, he sat on a bench in front of the hotel and tried to figure out where he could work. Obviously, his choices were limited.

Small wonder, then, that when word got around of the kind of money that was being shoveled out to NIL players during that 1948 to 1955 span, many pro ball players who were tiring of the minor league grind, and suspected they would never reach the majors, decided to jump ship and get in on the good semi-pro money while they still had the good baseball tools.

As for me, having been an art major at Nebraska, I wasn't sure where I could find financially and aesthetically satisfying employment. After a year at the Chicago Art Institute and my first summer with North Platte, I faced that problem. My rose-colored rookie glasses had been broken by the hard realities of small-town baseball economics. Gone was the excited, naive twenty-two-year-old who—as an avid reader of William Saroyan—viewed the town of McCook from a writer's distance, expecting Saroyan-like romances and magical chance contacts to take place between lonely, special people in the warm summer days as the lone meadowlark sang near the railroad tracks.

I was glad I had replaced those rose-colored glasses with shatterproof reality glasses, ground for the real world of baseball and life. They allowed me to see how to move on at the right time. Without this clear, soul-searching vision I might have drifted on in a Danny Farris–style journey fraught with anxiety, my best years discarded without significant memories. As it happened, my life took some unexpected and interesting turns away from the static and unproductive road it seemed to be following. At the end of the 1953 season I decided not to return to the NIL the following summer.

The sobering fact of the matter, though everyone in the NIL hoped it would go away, was that by about 1954, Hastings sportswriter Bill Madden's dire predictions and frantic warnings were coming true. Old Mother Hubbard's NIL cupboard was just about bare. The money needed to keep expensive baseball players just couldn't be found anymore. By the end of 1955 the stakes had gone so high in that mad poker game that everybody was having to fold.

I wasn't there to see it. I had taken a year to paint watercolors in Colorado Springs and wasn't sure where I would go after that. I did know that spending summers playing baseball in small, sleepy towns no longer seemed practical or even interesting. It had ceased to be fun and certainly wasn't helping me grow professionally in my interests outside baseball.

Even before I left, the mad whirl of NIL players switching teams for the highest offer was spinning in a circular frenzy, the players sensing the coming of the end and conducting their own wild "dance of death." Floyd Stickney, popular Kearney third baseman and manager, had left the Irishmen to manage Superior and help it field one of the league's best teams in the early 1950s. "King Kermit" Lewis, star slugger for Superior and later Holdrege, was talked into moving to North Platte for a bigger paycheck. The most surprising and drastic change was P. O. Karthauser—who to me was as solidly identified with the McCook Cats as Tommy LaSorda was with the Dodgers—switching to catch and manage the Holdrege Bears, the town that had once held official "Boo P. O. Karthauser" nights. And it went on and on, round and round, until "the merry-go-round broke down."

As the wheels were coming off the NILmobile, however, negotiations were taking place between major league owners and the bankrupt town baseball boards to try to salvage something. The major league owners wanted to start up a new minor league program at Class D level. It would be a rookie league, and the players would all presumably be eighteen to twenty years of age, each a scouted and signed top prospect.

Actually, the Class D idea had been considered as far back as 1948. But writers such as Jimmy Kirkman had warned North Platte citizens and others of the drawbacks of such a changeover; apparently it had been unsuccessfully tried years before in the old Nebraska State League. Devoted NIL fans too were skeptical of this plan because they knew the quality of baseball would take a few steps backward. Some expressed the fear that it would be only an extension of American Legion ball, which they already had. The fans who really knew baseball—and that included just about everybody except Mrs. Fagan, who was just too busy to follow sports—

were aware that the hitting and pitching and even fielding would not measure up to what the NIL had been providing.

What they couldn't ignore, though, was that this seemed to be the one saving plan to keep baseball without bankrupting the financially exhausted little towns that loved the game so much. The appealing part was that the major leagues would foot the entire bill for the operation if each town provided one thing: a good ballpark and grandstand. That alone would require substantial fund raising, but it seemed the only solution to keep live baseball alive in the area. So, in 1956 the six towns that had formed the NIL in 1955, its final season, plus Grand Island and Hastings, became homes for the new eight-team Class D Rookie League.

In his book *A False Spring*, Pat Jordan described his bittersweet experience in this new league as an eighteen-year-old pitcher with an outstanding fast ball who was signed by the Milwaukee Braves and sent to McCook for his rookie experience in 1959. Though he spent only two months in the town where I played the first three years of my NIL adventure, and pitched in a different ballpark, Jordan's descriptions of the southwestern Nebraska landscape and town life are sensitive and memorable. His penetrating accounts of time spent on the same streets and in the same cafés, walking the same sidewalks and sitting on the same hotel bench, just nine years after I left that special little town of eight thousand, are very meaningful to me personally.

I thought about the "baseball bums" I had known and wondered what they would all do after 1955. The Cornhusker League had been disbanded in 1953, and the Pioneer Nite League had shrunk to a four-team competition in 1955. With the NIL just suddenly gone, what would happen to all the good ballplayers who had made Tuesday, Thursday, and Sunday nights magical for those solid citizens hungry for quality baseball out there in the rural semi-pro baseball capital of the Midwest?

Television was making its way into a substantial number of homes as the NIL went under. The World Series was being broadcast (in black and white), and soon, many major and minor league ball games would be in the living rooms of all those McCook, North Platte, and other semi-pro enthusiasts. The baseball fans' world was changing more rapidly than they could have imagined. It was the passing of a truly unique and important time in rural America's sports history.

Don Hays

Stirring Some Hot-Stove Coals

In the spring of 1997 I wrote to the now retired Reverend Donald L. Hays about this book and asked him to send me some of his memories of the old NIL. I looked forward to his reply because forty-nine years earlier he had been McCook's third baseman, known as "little Donnie Hays" to McCook sports announcer Bob Morris, and Don or Donnie or D. Hays to other players. To me he was my little brother, who could really "pick it" and had a good enough arm to play (and had done so at different times) all the infield positions but first base. He had played third at McCook and second for Kearney during five of the years that I spent in the NIL. Here is most of what he wrote to me.

> My memories of playing for the Cats can't be separated from the vivid pictures, sounds and feelings of playing ball in the old East Park (or was it called Eastside Park?—just "East" sounds right to me). The crowd was right on top of you—in places an arm's length away.
>
> I remember playing third base—how it was an adventure when there was an overflow crowd spilling down the left field line—barely giving me (or Grogan) a chance to go after a pop fly in foul territory.
>
> And the sound of the ball off the bat—CRACK!—echoing around the wooden stands and fence! Remember some of those drives to right-center by McElreath? . . . he could really put wood on the ball.
>
> The infield, as I remember it, was well cared for (much bet-

ter than the later west side park), with fairly true hops. One memory which brings a smile to me (don't ask about dates or who we were playing): man on first; batter hits a screamer to my right—I throw my gloved hand across my body and somehow it is in my glove. Momentum carries me into a 360 degree turn and I am throwing to you at second and (my memory says) we complete the double play. That "vas vun from them goot memories"! [*Note:* This last sentence alluded to Eddie Miller's imitation of one of his German customers who often came into the grocery store and said, "Gif me sum from that goot chees."]

Grogan, of course, had the perfect nickname—Spider— and he could "work the web" (talk about being before one's time!) not only getting to the ball, but completing the play. What a pleasure it was to see how you two worked the double play! Speaking of double plays, did I ever send you the poem I wrote, titled "The 6–4–3 DP"? In case I didn't, I enclose a copy:

The Six-Four-Three DP

Tell me, friend, have you ever drunk deep, The ritual richness of, The Six-Four-Three DP?

The crowd is there, A blaring blur, Of Pitiless paper cups, Who Buy your time.

The score is locked, With one on, And one gone. The catcher signs to life, Univactivated moves Of a Defensive machine.

You and Bobby at short, Will think to the right, Knowing the wrong arm slant, Will be down and tight.

The stretch, And check, Starts your gentle Rocking, Timed to make you, Half a step better, Than you are.

The pitch. But damn! It's topped, Chopped, Past the pitcher, And, Bobby's flying in, While, Your feet have eyes, In their race, To second base.

All in one motion, Bobby's, Short-hop grab, And throw, While you know, That digging spikes, Are, Right on you!

No thought now—Leather! Wrist! Shock! Sky! Ground! Ringing sound! Got one! Was it two?

The quiet curses, Of the canceled runner, Sharing The taste of your dirt, Sound sweet, For they, Confirm completion, Of the Double Play.

Now you're up, And jogging, To the warmth, Of dugout grins. Bobby's at your side, Matching stride, In silent sign, Of sharing, The glow, Of knowing, How it's done.

—D. L. Hays

Tough pitchers to hit? My batting average would attest to the fact that most of them were tough for me. Does the term "banjo hitter" ring a bell? Strangely enough, the pitcher who seemed to give the guys the most trouble—Lefty Haines— was one I looked forward to facing. I would wait for his down-dropping curve ball and ride it to left (usually my pokes were to the right side). Funny thing—Floyd Stickney of the Irishmen taught me how to pull the ball (at last!). A simple move. When the pitcher rocked back, I would move the left knee in, naturally putting the bat in a cocked position. With the pitch, the bat, already cocked, only had to move forward.

You mention Billy Martin playing once for the Cats. It was a play-off game—and much as we were impressed with getting to be with a major leaguer, those of us who were benched felt some resentment—afterall, we had played the season and won enough games to get in the play-offs. At least I felt a little resentful (not toward Martin et al. but toward the management, who undoubtedly were influenced by the good old boys who had important bucks riding on the game). Martin didn't have a cap, so I volunteered mine (at least something of me was at the second base position!). He would have liked to borrow an arm as well, for his was so sore he could barely lob the ball to first. He hit well, including a remarkable shot over the deep right centerfield wall. I only remember one other Camp Carson import for that game—a slick fielding shortstop whose name I can't recall. I do remember that he had about the foulest mouth I'd heard (and, counting my Army experience, I had heard plenty).

Stirring Some Hot-Stove Coals · 203

Speaking of the Army—on the Second Army Team at Ft. Meade, in 1951 there were some outstanding players. There was Jim Lemon (the outfielder, not the pitcher) who played for the Senators and some other teams in the biggies. Hard to believe, but he hit at least as hard as Cerv, and harder than Horace Garner. There was Jim Rovner (Triple-A), with the fastest double play turn I've ever seen (live or on TV). Jim Brosnan, the Cub pitcher, who later would write one of the best baseball books I've read (I think it was called "The Long Season"). And you remember Carroll Beringer, the sneaky fast, very bright Double-A pitcher (played under Bobby Bragan at Fort Worth). And how could I forget Johnny Hrash, the Triple-A shortstop, who bumped me to the bench as soon as he arrived in camp.

You mention the Dollaghan incident. I look back and shake my head over the long-delayed usage of batting helmets. I am amazed at how few incidents of actual beanings we heard about. Was it because we didn't dig in, looking to drive the ball? Did most pitchers consciously opt to not be "head hunters"? I do know that I, because I stood close to the plate received my share of brush-back pitches, and some pitches landed in the middle of my back—none, fortunately, doing any significant damage.

Something to check out in your research: did Ernie Banks actually play some for Superior when he was about 17 years old? It's in my memory bank as an item. Is it true? [*Note:* From the 1982 *McCook Gazette* centennial edition: "Billy Martin, Tom Brookshier, Ernie Banks, Richie Ashburn, Ben Drieth . . . played for or against the old McCook baseball Cats, members of the Nebraska Independent League. The league was a confederation of teams whose players performed for pay at a level equal to the Class A minors." And "A young Ernie Banks, later a star for the Chicago Cubs, played third base for Superior."]

In Kearney, trying to play my way back into the lineup after my shoulder separation, playing North Platte I believe, I have a hot hitting night. After my third hit, I break up umpire Manley at first base when I say, "What does a guy have to do to break into this lineup?"

Also in Kearney, on a storm-threatening night, we are taking infield practice. The gathering crowd warily watches the gathering clouds and the flashes of lightning. I am thinking I would like to be somewhere under shelter when suddenly a bolt strikes one of the light standards and dances from pole to pole. With no discussion whatever, everybody—players and fans—are running for their cars. A wild storm ensues, and the game is washed out. My "respect for"—make that "creaturely fear of"—lightning is markedly increased, and to this day remains, only slightly diminished.

I remember those 90-plus miles per hour rides back to Mc-Cook from North Platte on only partly paved Highway 83, with Doc Dennis serenely aiming his big sedan southward, and somehow arriving safely and discharging his wide-eyed passengers.

I remember playing in Lexington when the Alfalfa processing plant was in full billow—the sickeningly sweet odor temporarily sapping enthusiasm for America's favorite pastime.

Lexington is also the locale for an episode which, when recalled, still impels me to hide my face in my nighttime pillow. It was a play-off game. Ben Dreith (the same guy who later became a top NFL official) is on the mound. I'm playing second. It's in the ninth inning, with one away and the winning run on third. The infield is drawn in and there is only one play on a ground ball—home. Dreith gets the batter to ground weakly toward me. I charge and come up with it. Somehow my visual calculations say that it will be too late to get the man at home, and I check my throw, and the game is over. Dreith goes ballistic. There was only one play! And I froze. It's silly that it still bothers me—but it does.

Images:
—Textbook swing: Donnie's big brother—Hobe
—Who you want in centerfield: Eddie Miller

—Who you want leading off: Bobby West

—Who you want in cleanup: Horace Garner

—Who you want blocking the plate: P. O. Karthauser

—Who you don't want up if you're playing third: Floyd Stickney

Undoubtedly, much more will surface as my memory uncovers this and that—and if it is significant I'll send it along.

Don and I were talking during his later visit to Lincoln, in 1998. "Where did you first hear the expression, 'Take two and hit to right'?" I asked.

"I don't know," Don replied. "It seems like I've heard it all my life. Where did you first hear it?"

"I think it was when I started playing with Sandy Silverio's team in 1946," I said. "I remember Sandy shouting it out, but I never knew exactly what it meant. I can't even remember the situation. What do you think it means?"

"Well—it could mean several things, I guess," Don said. "I think I first thought it meant, take two good swings and if you don't hit the long ball, choke up, guard the plate, and take the ball to right field. How about you?"

"I've thought some about it," I said. "It could mean, take two called strikes and then go the other way with the pitch, just getting some wood on it for a base hit. The point being, make the pitcher work, and still get the best of him by choking up and taking the ball the other way. You tire the pitcher and also demoralize him when you get a hit in the end. Or possibly it could be the hit-and-run— take two pitches, hoping the pitcher would get behind and have to come in with the third pitch for a strike, so you could get a good pitch to execute the hit and run to right field. Of course, if the pitcher threw two strikes, you're not in a good situation for a hit-and-run."

"This is very interesting. I wonder how many more we could think of?" Don said.

"Or, maybe it's only a decoy, to get the opposing pitcher confused," I went on. "If he thinks you are going to take two pitches, he might feel he can lay a couple right in there for strikes without you swinging. But then he might think, 'That's just what they want me to do, and then they will tee off on my fast ball.'"

"And you know what happens when ballplayers start thinking too much," Don said.

"Maybe that's all it was," I concluded. "Just something to mess with the mind."

"I think I like my first interpretation best," Don said.

"I believe I do too, after all this discussion," I said.

The question on the other end of the phone line came from Dr. Dave Garland, once one of the most confounding and winning right-handers in the NIL.

"Who was that guy who floored me?—I can't remember names—a stocky outfielder we had at McCook."

I hadn't seen or heard from Dave since we used to hang out in Mc-Cook together. My strongest memory was of Dave sitting at an old squeaky pump-organ in his rented apartment, playing a simple but beautiful rendition of "Poor Butterfly" while he waited for the chocolate cake he had whipped up to finish baking. I was on my way to work at the *Gazette* and needed some information for my column. He asked me if I wanted some cake, and I said, no, I just had breakfast.

My sources from McCook had told me in 1997 that Dave was still alive and living in Colorado. I looked in the phone book for his area and dialed a hit the first time. I told Dave of the book I was working on and we began reflecting.

"Floored you?" I repeated. "Stocky outfielder?" I thought quickly. "You mean Al McElreath?" He was the only one fitting the description.

"Yeah, McElreath! That's the guy."

"You mean he decked you? Slugged you?!" I said.

"Yes," Dave assured me. "Doc Dennis and Pat Patrick told me that year I managed—1949, I think—that Al was getting a little unpredictable and unreliable, and I would have to go get his uniform and release him."

"Happy Al punched you out?! I still can't believe it," I said. "I just remember him smiling and softly singing, 'I will be your rooster, if you'll be my hen. I'll come 'round and see you, every now and then.' And then he'd go up to the plate and rattle the fence with a double."

Dave continued, "I went down there with Horace Garner—he lived there too—to that apartment complex where Al and his family lived. I went up to him and said I was sorry, but I would have to ask for his uniform. That's all I remember. The next thing I knew I was looking up from the floor."

"The Muskogee Mauler!" I said. "He snuck one in on you, did he? Well, I'll be—"

"He didn't want to give me his uniform, that was clear."

I thought about Al. I never figured him to knock out his own playing manager. But the nomadic life of the semi-pro could wear on the nerves, and the yearly uncertainty put anyone on the edge. And a ballplayer's uniform was his living. It was the first time I had heard of the incident, though I had wondered what became of Al. This was one that slipped by the newspapers. Even Bill Madden had somehow missed it for his column in the *Hastings Tribune*.

"Do you know if Lefty Haines ever signed with any big league club?" I asked, deciding to change the subject. It was something I had wanted to know for a long time.

"I don't know," Dave said.

"How about Bill Gardner?"

"Don't know much about him either." Very few people had known anything about either of these two guys. They just seemed to come out at night under the lights, pitch you out of your socks, and then fade into the shadows. I wondered too about Walt Ibsen, who seemed to have been pitching around Holdrege forever.

"I was a 'bonus baby,' you know," Dave volunteered.

"I didn't know that."

"The St. Louis Browns wanted to sign me, but I had planned to go to medical school and didn't think I could play baseball at the same time. They asked me how much it would take to change my mind. I thought I would ask for something big, so I said, '$5,000,' a lot of money in 1940. They said okay and handed me a contract. So I tried doing both, but the second semester was a problem. I finally told them I just couldn't make it work," Dave explained.

With all of Garland's great stuff, I'd been sure some scouts must have been after him. And with his intelligence, I'd figured he would make it through medical school, which he did. He was team doctor for the Denver Broncos for a number of years and also for other Denver professional teams. In fact, when I talked to him in 1997, he was still practicing at age seventy-five: "I've worked all my life, and I'm still working."

I was impressed. "Dave," I said, "I need a photo of you around the time we played together. Just your face—I can supply the rest. I want you in the book, and I can't locate any picture of you."

"I don't know if I have one," Dave said. "I have a bunch of stuff in a box in the basement that I've been meaning to go through for years, but I've just been too busy."

"Well, now is the time, Dave. I'm saying some pretty good things about you in the book, and I want an illustration to go with it. I don't want to fake it from memory. I had to do that with my first sketch of Lefty Haines, and that's hard after forty-four years."

"I'll try to find one," he assured me.

I have in my memory a very clear image of Garland's pitching motion—that loose, Satchel Paige–like whipping arm action—and all his different speeds and movement on the pitches. I spent a lot of time looking over his left shoulder and marveling at the stuff the ball did from all those different points of release. Yet for some reason Dave's face isn't very clear in my mind anymore. Nor is Lefty's or Walt's or Art's. It must be that we hitters spend a lot more time looking right at their fingertips, the release point of the baseball, than at pitchers' faces.

Dave Garland

The Big East and the
Return to NILville

By March 1997 I was aware of a nostalgic urge to return to the scene of my baseball triumphs and other memorable moments in that mid-twentieth-century semi-pro experience. I had been away from the NIL since 1953, had played a few semi-pro games around Lindoln in 1955–56, and then starting in 1956 had served as the original full-time art director for University of Nebraska Educational TV (KUON-TV, then Channel 12) for six years. My wife, Bonna Tebo Hays, became the first paid woman director/manager of the Lincoln Community Theatre in 1960 at the age of twenty-two. In 1962 Bonna, also a fine actress, and I decided to head east to New York City to see what we could do in our respective fields of drama and art.

After trying the freelance art route for two years, and while Bonna was still appearing on TV soap operas in New York, I accepted the position of production designer and coordinator (also graphic artist and scene design instructor) for the theater department at Nassau Community College, a new and extremely ambitious educational institution in Garden City, on Long Island. With twenty-four thousand day and night students, NCC had an enormous production budget for the theater department through the 1960s and 1970s. The department's chairman, Wes Jensby, took full advantage of this and scheduled a year-round average of ten major productions. The facilities included not only an indoor stage but two large outdoor theaters where full-scale musicals were presented to thousands of Nassau County citizens per night in the summer.

Some of these productions employed famous stage and screen actors such as Kim Hunter, James Whitmore, Robert Ryan, and Ray Milland to act with the students.

Early in the spring semester of 1968, some of the acting students were playing a game of Wiffle ball on the grass between the theater offices and the stage. I noticed that the one pitching had a pretty good arm, so I went outside and asked to take a few swings myself. I could recognize a good throwing arm even with a Wiffle ball. Afterward, we began talking.

"You've played some baseball, haven't you?" I asked.

"Yeah, I've played some ball," the acting student said.

"Where?"

"Oh, Long Beach High. Before that, Little League, you know. I've had a few scholarship offers to smaller colleges in the Southeast."

"Second base?" I ventured, looking at his size.

"Shortstop," he corrected.

I told him I had played a little ball, too. College, semi-pro. He asked me where and I told him. He nodded with a look that had "not very impressed" written all over it. I had grown to know that look since coming east. Anything west of New Jersey was out of the loop. The Midwest, to New Yorkers and Long Islanders, was Ohio and Indiana; west of that they still rode shotgun on stagecoaches. But he was polite about it. He realized it wasn't my fault I didn't grow up "where it was happening."

"Who was your favorite major leaguer?" I asked. "You must have seen a lot of them as a kid."

"The Mick," he said, smiling. "Mickey Mantle."

We talked some more. He asked me what I taught. I recited my complete title and job description—new to NCC, a bit unusual, and I liked it. I told him I was also still painting and illustrating on the side. He asked me what I was working on, and I said a painting of Billie Holiday.

"I knew Billie," he said.

"You did? How?" I was impressed and surprised.

"She used to come to our house," the baseball-playing acting student said. My uncle owned Commodore and Blue Note records. Jazz artists were always hanging out at his house and at ours."

"Blue Note records!" It was like hearing the name of an old friend. "I spent many an hour sitting around on the floor of my college friend Bob Herbert's house back in Lincoln, Nebraska, listening to Blue Note records. Max Kaminsky, Art Hodes, and Mezz Mezzrow and the Chicago-style Dixieland jazz. Bunk Johnson and Sidney Bechet playing 'Days Beyond Recall' blues. In fact, I have a ten-inch LP of Billie which I think is Blue Note, and a Commodore twelve-inch LP of Eddie Condon's gang playing nothing but 'A Good Man Is Hard to Find.'"

One of the other Wiffle ball players came over to us. "Come on, Bill," he said. "We have to go rehearse," and they went inside to the stage.

"Bill?" I said, turning to another student. "What's his last name?"

"Crystal," he said. "Billy Crystal."

Billy Crystal was in many productions at Nassau Community College. The quality I first noticed about him was his extremely cool stage presence. Thinking about all the jazz recording artists hanging around his house ever since he was a baby, I could understand his lack of awe of famous people and his absence of stage fright.

In one of our summer productions—the 1940s musical *Finian's Rainbow*—we had Billy playing Og; Bill's older brother, Richard "Rip," who had a very fine baritone voice, playing Woody; and Bill's future wife, Janice Goldfinger, playing the pretty mute dancer, Susan. For a time Janice worked in the box office while Billy stayed home watching baby Jennifer and writing material for his stand-up routines at the clubs for new comics in New York City.

One day when I was talking to Billy and Janice in the box office, I mentioned a news item I had seen: "I read in the paper that they now have a new drug they can give to tall children who are growing too rapidly, which actually slows down the growth process and controls their height."

Billy looked at me with an absolutely straight face. "Yeah, that's what my parents had to do to me," he said.

I looked at him and had formed the word "really?" in my mouth before I caught up with him and realized he had suckered me completely. A grin crept over my face, and the corners of Billy's mouth moved into a wistful smile. From then on I was ready for his quick wit and the budding sense of humor that would take him so far in the entertainment field.

And then there was John Moschitta. Back when he was a little on the chunky side and acting in our NCC productions, I went into the men's rest room in the theater building one day and found him walking back and forth, talking to himself. (John appeared in the early 1990s television commercials as the thin man with the big eyes and little mustache who talked in "fast-forward" speed. In his student days he could do the whole "Trouble in River City" number from *Music Man* in thirty seconds or less.)

Noticing that John was wearing only his shorts, I said, "What's the matter, John, did you lose your pants?"

"Should I, or shouldn't I?" John mumbled, still pacing rapidly back and forth.

"Should you what?" I said.

"The guys bet me fifty bucks I didn't have the nerve to streak across the street to the cafeteria at class break," he said. "They all pooled their money."

To those who are too young to remember or just weren't paying attention, "streaking" was a strange ritual of the 1970s in which a person would make a short dash at full speed, completely naked, among surprised and possibly shocked observers. For example, an unclad young drunk raced across one of the greens in the British Open and was brought down with a solid tackle by PGA golfer Peter Jacobsen after the bobbies failed to do the job.

"Well, John," I began in my best fatherly wisdom voice, "think about it carefully. You will have to live with this, you know."

"Fifty bucks!" John said. We both pondered the choice, I motionless and John walking in circles around me. Suddenly, as the class bell rang, John stepped out of his shorts, exclaimed "I'm going!" and raced outside. I heard shouts and laughter, and then car horns and squealing brakes, and I knew chubby John had done the fifty-yard dash across the street. I hoped he knew about the side door that led to some seldom-used rooms before you got to the cafeteria itself. I never asked him. I do know one lady almost hit a tree in swerving up onto the curb when John's sprinting body flashed in front of her car.

It was years later, after I'd retired and we'd moved back to Lincoln, Nebraska, in 1995, that I began working on this book. During days in the Nebraska Historical Society microfilm room and at the drawing board, a parade of diamond ghosts drifted by. As I wrote about and illustrated images from my now reappearing semi-pro and college baseball past, I developed an increasing hunger to revisit those fading sites of NIL excitement before they were buried deep in real estate or highway development. My fear was that I might already be too late. Had I pushed this whole section of my life so far back on the shelf that my newfound interest in revisiting it had missed its moment?

I had to give it a try. We had planned a family trip to Denver, so I mapped out stopovers at Holdrege and McCook on the way out and at North Platte, Lexington, and Kearney on the way back. Except for Superior, which was too far out of the way, these made up the core NIL. Only time would tell what, if anything, would be left as standing evidence of my own "fields of dreams."

We drove into Holdrege from the north on the first day of spring 1997—forty-four years since the last time. I tried to remember where the ballpark was located. I had a feeling it was south of town. After driving around a little and looking for tall light poles, I stopped at a Casey's convenience store and asked the oldest clerk I could find if she knew of any such park still standing. She gave us directions to a ball field south and east which sounded like what we were after.

When we pulled up behind the backstop, I looked over the long rows of wooden bleachers and was sure I had been there before. The park faced east with the sun setting behind the bleachers. This felt right. I went out on the diamond to home plate and took my stance with my invisible thirty-four-inch Joe Cronin, waiting for Walt Ibsen's first pitch. My daughter Alison stood by the mound and snapped a picture of me as I took the pitch for a strike on the outside corner. Then I walked eagerly to the second-base area, now covered with thin sprouts of brown grass.

"This is exactly where I played!" I said, bending over with my hands on my knees and smiling. I heard the crack of the bat, and left-handed hitter Herschel Rinehart lined a one-hopper down the third-base line, a sure double. But "little Donnie Hays," not playing him to pull, stabbed the ball with the web of his glove, spun completely around, and fired it to me as I raced to cover. I whipped it on to Gene Dellenbach at first for a double play, and the bleacher ghosts groaned in Holdrege frustration while Rinehart kicked the dirt beyond first base and cursed. It had happened right here forty-nine years earlier. Alison snapped another shot of me relaying the pivot over a real second base still left out on the diamond.

I jogged over to where Donnie had picked that smash and rounded third slowly toward home.

"Man!" I said, looking at the distant home plate, "that's a long way down there. It used to be shorter!" I remembered the thrill of flying around third at full speed on a base hit and sliding home to score. I thought about big Walt Charlesworth, catcher and manager of the Bears, waiting for the throw while I hoped it would be off line.

McCook was the next stop—where it all started. We checked into a motel very close to the railroad station, and I went in to get some information. From the outside the station appeared less than prosperous. On the inside it was an all but deserted shell. It was only four-thirty in the afternoon, but there was no sign of life. Then I heard a voice behind the door in the back room. I knocked and a man of about forty-five opened the door. He was alone. He had been on the telephone.

"Is this the ticket office?" I asked.

"There is no official ticket office," he said. "Amtrak stops once in a while to drop off and pick up a few passengers, but there is no regular train run through here anymore."

"I came out here in 1948 on the Burlington train to play baseball in the NIL," I said. "Now I'm revisiting the old ballparks, but I'm having trouble finding them."

"Well," the station operator said, "the old Fairgrounds Park has been completely built over into a complex of softball fields and junior baseball. The old Eastside has been downsized to a Little league park, but it's still in the same place."

After inspecting the new Fairgrounds sports complex out northwest of town, we drove over to find the new Eastside Park, now called Felling Field. At East Seventh Street the ball field suddenly appeared before us, an eerie imitation of the old diamond we'd started out on forty-nine years before. From a distance the outfield fence seemed the same, but closer examination showed it to be a scaled-down replica; it was not as high and had been moved in much closer so that young players could hit the ball over it. Brightly painted messages about town merchants had been reproduced from the old days, though, in an attempt to preserve the legendary charm of the original battlefield of so many early NIL classics. It was really the only standing baseball reminder of my early memories of McCook.

No grown-up baseball. No NIL. No Kansas-Nebraska, Big Three, Nebraska State, or even Class D Rookie League ball. No kind of baseball older than American Legion to call the fans to the parks on those warm, exciting evenings. No times to sit beside your neighbor and roar in collective pride over a sudden athletic success of your "town" team. Now there were only network TV images, far removed and sanitary, viewed over couch-potato contours. I felt depressed at the loss and sad for those who would never taste that real baseball world of dirt and wool and hear the live echoing crack of a ball hit with wood-solid force in a wood-fenced ballpark.

"There just isn't any adult league baseball active anymore in McCook," the Amtrak sentry had said with resignation. "The town hasn't really grown much in all these years. The population went up to about eleven thousand for a while, but then it went back down. It's only about eight thousand now." I smiled at that.

"Do you know what the population was when I came out here in 1948?" I answered for him: "The sign by the station here said, 'McCook—pop. 8,000.'"

No more town baseball. The words kept coming back. We walked to our car, and a meadowlark warbled its lonely song from the top of a telephone pole. I remembered walking along the railroad tracks on warm, distant summer mornings just a few yards from this spot and hearing the same song. The meadowlark was one thing I could still count on. It, at least, made a happy contact with my world of forty-nine years before, which until now had seemed deserted and bleak on this windy day in late March.

We drove slowly by the old *Gazette* newspaper building with its narrow front and its stone-chiseled letters at the top: "19 Gazette 26." It was the year I was born. We drove around some more. I tried to find Mrs. Pearl Fagan's house where I roomed with brother Don for several years. I must have passed it, but I couldn't be sure which house it was.

On Norris Avenue between First and Second Streets on the north side of an old brick building were peeling, white letters spelling "Pat's Booterie—Fine Shoes." Pat Patrick's shoe store—I had once gone there to collect my reward when I lined a double off the right center sign that said, "Hit me and win a new pair of shoes."

Having supper at the Country Kitchen near our motel later, I stared moodily out the front windows as the ever-charging eighteen-wheelers rumbled through town on Highway 6, taking something somewhere. Semi-pro baseball was a memory only for the old in McCook. Town baseball for men was now dusty history, like gunfighters and real cowboys. There were no more wooden signs at downtown intersections saying, "Baseball Tonight."

A week later we blew (literally) into North Platte, racing a dust storm to the north of us on I-80. At one point a miniature tornado confronted us with violently spinning tumbleweeds; it failed to take us to the Land of Oz but did make staying on the highway an adventure. After slowly grinding our way through the little twister, a claustrophobic experience not unlike a tumbleweed car wash, we checked into the Hampton Inn south of town. We braced ourselves into the dust storm toward Applebee's sixty yards away and had a good meal. Then we headed into downtown North Platte, hoping to enjoy old landmarks. I didn't recognize anything. I turned on Sixth Street and headed for Jeffers Avenue, turning north again over the viaduct above the train tracks. To our left below I should have seen

Jeffers Field, but instead a crowded group of granaries met my gaze. The old ballpark had been replaced by a more commercial use of space.

I was told about Cody Park, a mile or so farther north and a few blocks west of Jeffers. That must have been where the Class D Rookie League, which took over in 1956, played its games and where Pat Jordan pitched for the McCook Braves. My chances of finding anyone old enough to tell me what happened to Jeffers Field at this time of day were very slim, so I decided I would have to trace the demise of my old friend back at the microfilm library at the Nebraska State Historical Society.

Of the three NIL towns revisited so far, North Platte seemed the most complete stranger. Only on Sixth Street did I get a feeling of having been there before. Driving around town, I saw little that was familiar and had no sense of returning. No recognition of buildings as in McCook. No song of a meadowlark from the top of a telephone pole. I listened carefully but no plaintive voice of Eddie Arnold guided me to the location of the little café where I once drank coffee and sustained my loneliness with strains of "Born to Lose." Where had I once painted bucking broncos on storefront windows before the rodeo? Sixth Street! That's what it was! I had decorated a couple of windows with bucking broncos on that street near Jeffers. I had been out there two days after I was beaned, going from store to store a little dizzy and with a slight headache, to get them done before the rodeo hit town.

In driving around trying to jump-start my lagging memory, I remembered that sunny morning in front of Hinman's Motors, waiting with Bob Harris and Tommy O'Connor for the appearance of the parade that kicked off the rodeo. Suddenly I'd heard the clarion call from a cornet driving like nobody else in history—Bix charging through the truck speakers with "At the Jazz Band Ball." It gave me goose bumps to hear Bix Beiderbecke strutting his stuff way out here in Buffalo Bill town. I, in my jazz conceit, had been certain I was the only one there at that moment who even knew of this jazz legend. Anyway, this unexpected aspect of the rodeo parade had caused a lonely and slightly displaced artist to smile the rest of the day, something I had not been accused of doing for some time.

Back on the road again, we were beginning to tire. Lexington would be a brief stop. The ball field, I was certain, would by now be plowed under and part of somebody's farm, or the alfalfa plant. We drove around briefly, trying to stir memories and recognize something, but it had been too many years.

I pulled into a car dealership and asked if anyone knew about the ballpark. Patient salespeople looked politely at me between phone calls. Then one wrote a name on a business card and handed it to me.

"I really can't help you," she said, "but he can, if anyone in this town can."

I looked at the card. "Thanks," I said. It read, "Bill Denker," my old infield buddy from the University of Nebraska and NIL days. Then we drove on. I would get in touch with Bill when we got back to Lincoln. I could get his telephone number from the alumni office.

We headed east for our last stop, Kearney. The Irishmen's old bleachers would be there, I was absolutely certain—maybe forever, because like historical amphitheaters the Kearney seats were built for the ages: they were solid steps of concrete on the side of a hill. I doubted if anyone had attempted to remove them since I was last here.

I was right. The field was just as I'd left it forty-four years before. In fact, the diamond was freshly dragged and chalk-lined, ready for a game between the University of Nebraska at Kearney and Moorhead State University from Minnesota. But the weather intervened. The frigid March wind blustered across the empty concrete rows with such chilling force that the game was called, and the shivering ballplayers filed, jacket-clad and high-shouldered, into the team bus.

My trusty camera girl, Alison, gamely aimed her lens into the teeth of the gale and got off a few slightly out-of-focus, windblown shots before repairing with haste to the warmth of the car. It was not a day for the national pastime. But it was good to know that this solid park had survived intact. The field looked as good as ever and was obviously used for frequent high school, American Legion, or college games, if not the legendary contests of a long-gone semi-pro era.

Bill Denker was at home in Lexington when I reached him by phone a few days after we arrived back in Lincoln. We had not talked since NIL days, and we had a lot to remember.

"One pitcher I had trouble with—I don't know if many others did, but I certainly did—was Chuck Eisenman," Bill said.

"The big right-hander with Kearney who had the huge German Shepherd?"

"That's the guy," Bill said. "His curve ball was always dropping off out in front of me. I never could hit it solidly."

"I would chase it clear across the plate to the other batter's box," I said. "I know exactly what you mean. It looked so good, but I could never reach it. What a tight spin it had! And then he would throw that fast one by you inside."

"And Max Quick," Bill went on. "He threw hard—real hard—and was tough to hit under those lights." We both reflected on those two NIL aces for a moment. "And speaking of Eisenman's big dog," Bill continued, "do you know *Life* magazine came in and did a whole story on Chuck and his dog? With some players and Ed Manley— Manley lived in McCook, didn't he?"

"Yes, he did," I recalled. "Umpire Ed with the cigar stub. Eddie Miller used to shout, 'Who told you, Manley?' after he made a strike call."

"They staged the whole picture spread with Ed and the dog chasing him and everything. Chuck really had that dog trained. You know it was one of those trained dogs that starred in some TV show, like Lassie."

My thoughts came back again to the Lefty Haines question.

"You would know, Bill, if anyone does," I began, "if Lefty Haines ever signed with any major league club when he was young."

"I'm not sure," Bill said. "Lefty was a different kind of guy, you know. Nobody knows much about him. He would be leaning against a streetlight or sitting on the steps before a game by himself, while the rest of us were together talking. He just drove to the ballpark in that little black pickup, pitched the game, and drove home with his pitching arm out the window and his short-sleeve shirt rolled up over his shoulder. He never put a jacket on that arm when he drove home. But I don't think he ever had a sore arm."

"I think the cool breeze driving home must have felt good on his arm," I said. "He was just ahead of his time—now they ice the arm after a game. They don't even try to keep it warm like in the old days."

"I think you're right," Bill agreed. "I think that's what it was. Lefty knew how to take care of his arm." Bill paused a moment. "About Lefty signing—I do remember hearing somewhere that he once drove to Oklahoma City to sign with someone, but when he got to the hotel, he decided to turn around and go home. Lefty was a shy guy, a loner."

We both thought about Lefty and his quiet, private behavior. "You know," I continued, "I always had trouble hitting him, but one day, that year when he pitched for Kearney, I drilled his curve hard to left field. When I came up to bat the next time, he knocked me down with the first pitch. And I mean it was close!"

"Lefty?" Bill laughed. "The pitch must have got away from him. I never saw him throw at anyone."

But I remembered that after the knockdown pitch Lefty had put his hands on his hips and made a face as if to say, "How do you like that, wise guy?" If Haines was such a nice guy, he had a funny way of showing it. Then I remembered telling the first baseman, after the line drive, that it was the first solid hit I'd had off Lefty in about two years. Since I was smiling when I said it, Lefty might have seen it and thought I was gloating. Or possibly the first baseman had said something to Lefty in the dugout—that I didn't think much of his curve, or worse.

I think I sensed the gap in purpose and intensity between local town players and players like me (outside mercenaries) during my playing days, but not until long afterward did I fully understand the size and personal impact of that gap. Now, I am certain there had to have been some resentment of my transient noninvolvement. The luxury of being able simply to show up at the ballpark and play the game for the fun of the game, without the constant burden of coming through for the hometown, must have been envied and eventually resented. While being aware of the fiscal needs of the Baseball Board, and each town's anxiety around Shaughnessy playoff time, I never felt personally responsible.

Certainly, it never really occurred to me that all this fun and baseball adventure might suddenly be canceled. The NIL seemed strong enough to withstand outside detractors and inside fiscal shortages simply because I wanted it to be. I existed day to day as if I could play in the league as long as I was happy doing it and, when I wasn't anymore, could just move on to something else in my life. Many players did not have that kind of freedom. Looking back, I believe this undoubtedly affected the feelings of some of them toward me.

Bill Denker and I switched to talk of other players.

"Grogan," I began. "Do you know what happened to Bob Grogan? I called the alumni office and the athletic office, and neither one had an address for him."

"I tried to locate Bob myself once," Bill said. "He just seems to have disappeared. You know, he was kind of a private guy himself. He never said much."

"He had a soft voice out there in the infield and I had trouble hearing what he said. But you were right next to him too—do you remember him saying something to the pitcher like 'wheedle deedle, wheedle deedle'?"

"No, I don't remember that," Bill said. "I don't remember Bob saying anything. And he was kind of a hard guy to get to know."

"Well," I continued, "I used to hear him saying that softly just before the pitch, and I'd think, 'What the hell *is* that?' I finally figured out he was saying to the pitcher, 'Wheel and deal it, wheel and deal it.'"

A few days after that conversation with Bill Denker, I found out what had happened to the Jeffers ballpark. Talking with our neighbor Byron Boslau, who had grown up in North Platte, I asked if he knew anything about it.

"Oh, it burned down," Byron said, "back in the '60s. I was delivering papers on my bike one day and I saw smoke, and we all rushed over to see what it was."

So that's what happened, I thought. That old infield compounded of switch-engine soot and Platte River silt was buried in an even more complex mixture with the addition of grandstand ashes.

At that moment my mind skipped back to sure-handed, smooth-throwing Holdrege shortstop Tom Sutak, mixing a little foxtrot with his crow-hop as he took infield practice at old Jeffers Field to the pregame music from the announcer's booth. His smile became wider as Yank Lawson's driving trumpet electrified all those who felt the special ensemble thrill of perfectly meshed Dixieland blues. I know there were two people there that night who never heard "Five Point Blues" sound so good: the foxtrotting Holdrege shortstop and the Plainsmen's second baseman. It was one of those special times when you feel, if only for a brief moment, a wave of harmony and completeness and wish life could give you more such moments.

Almost half a century later I still look back on those times with pride and fondness. I forget about the hours of boredom and loneliness. I discount the tense, underlying feuds between certain towns and players as the costs got out of hand, feuds that took the "boy" out of baseball and put the "hired gun" into it. Instead, I can get goose bumps remembering that incredible first-year roar after I relayed a ball from Bob Grogan to make a double play that killed a Holdrege rally in the late innings of a 1948 playoff game. More than 3,500 fans were squeezed into the 1,500-seat Eastside ballpark, hundreds sitting along the third- and first-base lines and inside the fence behind the surprised outfielders.

My slow-motion trot to the dugout after that relay to first was a dreamlike, out-of-body experience, the like of which I have never felt at any other time. With each step the volume of the crowd roar seemed to change, as if someone had a hand on the volume control and were turning it up and down in cadence with my stride. I cannot imagine any Rookie League game generating such an explosive release of stifled town pride, relief, and collective sports joy in a sound that must have been heard all the way to Holdrege. It was as close as I have ever felt to being swept up and carried on the shoulders of sound waves in a numbing, surreal moment of pure sports triumph.

It was a great ride, bumpy and shaky at times, but I wouldn't have missed it for the world.

Appendix

Nebraska Semi-Pro Leagues
Team Standings and
Starting Lineups, 1948

TEAM STANDINGS

Nebraska Independent League

McCook (Cats)	17 and 3
Kearney (Irishmen)	14 and 6
Holdrege (Bears)	10 and 10
Superior (Knights)	9 and 12
North Platte (Plainsmen)	8 and 13
Lexington (Minutemen)	3 and 17

Pioneer Nite League

Southern Division

Fremont	17 and 3
Stromsburg	12 and 7
Schuyler	11 and 8
Wahoo	7 and 11
David City	6 and 13
Columbus	4 and 15

Northern Division

Pender	19 and 1
Wayne	11 and 9
Wakefield	9 and 9
Blair	7 and 11
West Point	5 and 13
Tekamah	4 and 12

Cornhusker League (as of July 30)

York	14 and 2
Seward	9 and 6
Utica	8 and 7
Sutton	7 and 8
Osceola	6 and 7
Aurora	6 and 8
Geneva	5 and 10
Central City	4 and 11

STARTING LINEUPS

Abbreviations:

pitcher	p
catcher	c
shortstop	ss
first base	1b
second base	2b
third base	3b
left field	lf
center field	cf
right field	rf

Nebraska Independent League

McCook (Cats)

3b	Don Hays
2b	Hobe Hays
1b	Gene Dellenbach
ss	Bob Grogan
lf	Al McElreath
rf	Babe Fidler
c	P. O. Karthauser
cf	Eddie Miller
p	Bill Gardner
p	Ed McCarthy

Other McCook players, 1948–55: Anderson, Don (p); Andrew, Bob (ss); Ansley, Ed (cf); Babb, Fred (lf); Bacon, Don (3b); Baxter, Jack (1b); Begeman, Augie (p); Bergman, Don (p); Bernardi, Frank (rf); Boeger, Ross (2b); Brenning, Wally (p); Brookshire, Tom (p); Burgess, Bill (1b); Carlson, Don (p); Conboy, Jim (p); Craig, Myron (ss); Curry, Lacy (3b); Decker, Bob (2b); Dembricki, Stan (c-ss); Distefano, Paul (rf); Dunaway, Marv (lf); Finnegan, Phil (1b); Garland, Dave (p); Garner, Horace (rf); Gaston, Joe (p); Germano, Ralph (p); Goenst, Charles (cf); Haggerty, Pat (2b); Harmon, George (p); Horine, Larry (rf); Hull, Rex (3b); Jensen, Bill (ss); Johnson, Bill (lf); LaMagna, Joe (rf); Leach, Carl (p); Lubin, Danny (p); Lukas, Mike (1b); Maglie, Bob (cf); Manley, Bob (p); Martin, Billy (2b); McCarthy, Charles (1b); McCoy, Bennie (p); McKillip, Leo (c); Mohorcick, Joe (lf); Moranville, Ken (p); Moss, Marion (p); Moyer, Gaylen; Nagel, Fran (ss); Nuckolls, Darrell; Opperman, Dan (p); Parker, Galen (1b); Phillips, Buddy (c); Rego, Johnny (ss); Schleissler, Ted (c); Schoonmaker, Bob (3b); Sharp, Jim (cf); Stearns, Bill (c); Stevens, Jim (1b); Stubblefield, Mickey (p-2b); Sutak, Tom (ss-3b); Taylor, Gene (rf); Tocky, Jack (p); Trofholz, Sook (lf); Van Nordheim, Ed (p); Verenoult, "Boz" (c-ss); Vukas, Steve (p); West, Bob (rf); Willingham, John (p); Wollard, Jim (3b); Wollenweber, Art (p)

Kearney (Irishmen)	
cf	Skeeter Payne
ss	Del Harris
1b	Harvey Daake
3b	Floyd Stickney
2b	Gerald Peterson
c	Dode Graham
rf	George Binger
lf	Tom Guilfoyle
p	Walt Ibsen
p	Frank Sajavec
p	Paul Hiller

Other Kearney players, 1948–55: Babbit (2b); Berg, Ed (2b); Bogue, Russ (lf); Burkhart, John (c); Eisenmann, Chuck (p); England, Fred (cf); Gifford, Ron (ss); Gill, Bobby (p); Grassmeyer, Jerry (1b); Harnegal, Lee (rf); Hays, Don (2b); Henderson, Oakie (p); Hulsebus (ss); Johnson, Ray (cf); Knickerum, Bob (lf); Lavery, Haig (1b); Meyers, Dick (c); Moore, Jerry (ss); Myers, Ken (c); Neil, Dick (c); Perry, Paul (lf); Reaugh, Jim (cf); Roh, Roman (p); Roth, Tom (1b-c); Sintek, Wayne (lf); Staab, Ed (p); Thesnega, Jug (p); Thorell, Stu (c); Tismerat, John (p); Wagonhurst, Chuck (p); Wilcox, Jack (ss); Womack, Moose (1b)

Holdrege (Bears)

2b	Herschel Rinehart
lf	Dale Meisenbach
p	Art Dollaghan
c	Ken Strong
cf	Ray Johnson
rf	Al Bienhoff
1b	Ray Olson
3b	Carlos Hansen
ss	Hal Marks

Other Holdrege players, 1948–55: Baxter, Jack (1b); Becher, Bill (3b); Bloomfield, Jimmy Joe (lf); Brockhaus, Jim (2b); Brose, John (p); Bruner, Jack (1b); Cederdahl, Jim (cf); Charlesworth, Walt (c); Distefano, Bob (2b); Distefano, Paul (c); Dunbar, Fay (lf); Fields, Stroud (p); Finley, Earl (c); Giles, Bill (1b); Hardy, Carol (cf); Harmson, Mike (p); Hawkins, Len (cf); Hotton, Rich (3b); Ibsen, Walt (p); Johnson, Ben (rf); Jones, Bill (lf); Kuhns, Gene (cf-1b); Larson, Don (ss); Lewis, Kermit (1b); Lott, Bobby (2b); Majors, Jim (1b); McCormick, Gary (p); McKillip, Leo (c); Nevins, Marv (c); Paulson, Bob (c); Poff, Shirley (p); Quick, Max (p-lf); Reynolds, Bob (2b-lf); Rissoli, Harry (cf); Rolston, Dirkes (ss); Salberg, Chris (ss-p); Sanders, Dick (ss); Shirley, Bob (p); Spearman, Kirk (p); Stickles, Chuck (3b);

Stickney, Bob (c); Sutak, Tom (ss); Swanson, Bob (p); Taft, Bob (3b); Wells, Bob (p); Wilkening, Bill (cf)

Superior (Knights)

cf	Bill DeLozier
3b	Ed Stewart
2b	Don Taylor
1b	Kermit Lewis
lf	Sam Somerhalder
rf	Dave McLaughlin
c	Don Maul
ss	Jerry Koch
p	Lon Kubat

Other Superior players, 1948–55: Bart, Hal (ss); Bethel, Mickey (p); Boyd, Bob (lf); Buckley, Johnny (ss); Creedon, Connie (rf); Davis, Don (c); Dockins, George (p); Gilchrist, Verdon (ss); Graves, Gene (c); Harder, Ted (rf); Harmson, Bill (p); Hein, Val (lf); Hurd, Tommy (p-ss); Isert, Lon (c); Kipp, Fred (p); Lawson, Al (p); McClain, Pat (p); McDonald, Merrill (1b); McMahon, Jim (p); Nicolai, Mel (p); Paniak, Joe (p); Romano, Lee (ss); Sampson, Roy (lf); Sepich, Matt (2b); Shogren, Danny (1b); Snyder, Rus (rf); Stetzel, Pete (1b); Stickles, Chuck (ss); Stickney, Floyd (3b); Sunblad (1b); Tickel, Leo (ss); Trujillo, Ernie (p); Williams, Hank (p); Wilson (p); Wolfenbarger, Ben (rf); Wonka, Casey (cf); Young, Eldon (rf)

North Platte (Plainsmen)

rf	Bill McCowin
ss	Whitey Kurkowski
c	Bob Paulson
cf	Butch Neiman
lf	Paul Ward
3b	Del Bailor

1b	Marvin Homan
2b	Paul Barraclough
p	Lefty Mazell

Other North Platte players, 1948–55: Adzik, Nick (c); Anderson, Clyde (p); Austin, Bob (3b); Backhaus, Murray (c); Bennett, Ron (3b); Best, Bill (p); Bowes, Mason (p); Burges, Bob (1b); Callaghan, Jim (p); Chehey, Max (ss); Coufal, Irv (lf); Denker, Bill (3b); Dreffs, Marvin (p); Dunn, Clayton (c); Dunn, Jerry (rf); Frisina, Joe (2b); Harris, Bob (3b); Hawkins, Len (lf); Hays, Hobe (2b); Hegwood, Fritz (lf); Henton, Dick (p); Hopp, Johnny (1b); Hunt, Ray (3b); Johnson, Ken (p); Kitamura, Dick (2b); Knopka, Bruno (1b); Lebedz, George (ss); Lewis, Kermit (1b); Mason, Warren (p); Mathis, John (p); O'Connor, Tom (c); Odren, Dick (2b); Ossino, Angelo (p); Peck, Jack (rf); Pederson, Dave (p); Powley, Buzz (rf); Quick, Max (p-lf); Richardson, Don (3b); Straub, Don (p); Swanson, Bob (p); Thuman, Lucky (3b); Tolly, Roscoe (c); Trapp, Al (lf); Walter, Dale (lf); Wells, Fred (p); Wright, Thurman (1b); Young, Lane (c)

Lexington (Minutemen)

2b	Shean
1b	Al Ourada
3b	Ray Simmons
cf	Irv Coufal
lf	Smith
rf	Ingram
c	Roe
ss	Ike Southerland
p	Lefty Haines

Other Lexington players, 1948–55: Andrews, Bob (ss); Barrett, Red (p); Bennett, Ron (cf); Cerv, Bob (cf); Cordell (rf); Craig, Myron (ss); Denker, Bill (3b); Fitzgerald, Bill (rf); Low, Wayne (1b); McCardle, Ken (c); Neil, Chuck (p); Neiman, Butch (cf); Novak, Ray (p); Papolio (2b); Pesba, Tommy (rf); Rego, Johnny (ss); Risinger, Don (rf); Rolston (ss);

Seger, Fred (1b); Thune, Al (p); Warren, Pee Wee (2b); Workington, Conrad (c)

Grand Island (Islanders)
(played in the NIL in 1949 only)

2b	Al Karle
lf	Bob Reynolds
rf	Bob Maiden
cf	Ray Johnson
1b	Tank Cambell
c	Walt Charlesworth
ss	Jerry Koch
3b	Huck Johnson
p	Art Dollaghan

Other Grand Island players, 1949: Bryant (2b); Kaeding, Jim (ss); Knickrehm, Bob (1b); Maiden, Bob (ss); Nelson, Doug (lf); Stroh, Rollie (rf), Trieshman, Art (p)

Hastings (Sultans)
(played in the NIL in 1949 only)

lf	Dick Crabtree
1b	Chuck Stickles
c	Byron Boals
2b	Roy Strong
3b	Pete Stoetzel
ss	Duane Peterson
rf	Felps
cf	Rose
p	Ed Van Nordheim

Other Hastings players, 1949: Dannells, Everett (p); Gaston, Tom (p); Kueck, Russell (lf); Maul, Don (c); McQuiston (p); Patzer (2b); Van Pool, Jack (1b); Yung, Eldon (1b)

Pioneer Nite League

Southern Division

Fremont

ss	George Gribble
p	Eddie Stanek
3b	Mahacek
cf	Peterson
1b	Draemel
2b	Parsons
c	Jaksick
lf	Launer
rf	Christensen

Stromsburg

1b	Gerry
rf	Long
c	Sullivan
p	Quick
3b	Bond
lf	Johnson
ss	Willets
2b	Wolfe
cf	Ehlers

Schuyler

2b	Trofholz
3b	B. Stickney
ss	Faltys
c	Larson
rf	Bogner
lf	Van Ackeran
1b	Oberg
cf	Morbach
p	Hiller

Wahoo

1b	Petrzelka
lf	Saunders
3b	Denker
ss	Schlesinger
cf	Cerv
c	Kubat
rf	McGill
2b	Ohnouta
p	Weigert

David City

rf	Hunsche
cf	Oksina
2b	Kreiszinger
ss	Sharpe
3b	Hafemeister
c	Armagost
1b	Schleiger
lf	Roh
p	B. Meysenburg

Columbus

1b	Van Ackeran
ss	Jensen
lf	Weiser
cf	Herrod
2b	Pilfold
3b	Baumgart
c	Wertz
rf	Tarczon
p	Czopa

Northern Division

Pender

1b	Johnson
2b	Bull

ss	Kroger
3b	Grant
rf	Tigh
cf	Powley
lf	Repschlager
c	Blatchford
p	Ossino

Wayne

ss	Webber
rf	Bahe
lf	Moyer
2b	Griesch
p	Kimmel
cf	Johnson
c	Harder
1b	Page
3b	Sherlock

Wakefield

cf	Brownlee
lf	Lammers
rf	Ellyson
c	J. Anderson
2b	Sckolowski
1b	B. Erickson
ss	Burlage
3b	D. Erickson
p	Schroer

Blair

rf	Robinson
ss	Steward
cf	Wolff
3b	Dickerson
1b	Scoles
c	Peterson

lf	Stork
2b	Megrue
p	Gresham

West Point

cf	Peterson
1b	Wegner
2b	Diers
rf	Battenhorst
lf	Schmidt
3b	McGill
ss	Buchols
c	Duda
p	Ostramic

Tekamah

2b	Lemaster
1b	J. Meggal
ss	Fitch
c	Smagacz
3b	Beard
cf	Rosaeker
rf	L. Jackson
lf	J. Erickson
p	Conklin

Cornhusker League

York

ss	G. Kaeding
1b	Campbell
cf	W. Kaeding
3b	B. Graff
lf	Schneider
rf	Isaacs
2b	M. Kaeding
c	B. Kaeding
p	Neujahr

Osceola

lf	Schmoker
1b	Lamb
c	Bond
2b	Sterup
rf	Bruckner
p	Blessie
ss	Mickey
3b	Johnson
cf	Henggeler

Utica

2b	C. Baack
1b	C. Reiling
3b	D. Neujahr
lf	Schmieding
ss	Booker
c	Boals
rf	V. Baack
cf	Marting
p	Halfmeister

Geneva

3b	McClusky
ss	Becker
cf	M. Bornschlagel
3b	Sharkey
rf	Kamler
1b	Curtis
c	McDonald
p	J. Bornschlagel

Seward

rf	Rickel
2b	Kessler
ss	Hungerford
3b	Hofmeister

c	Rublee
1b	Neiman
lf	Reiling
p	Schaepler
cf	Walker

Aurora

lf	Topham
3b	Tyre
ss	Hartzell
cf	Smith
2b	Mitchell
rf	D. Enderle
1b	R. Enderle
c	Fenster
p	Korte

Sutton

3b	Stetzel
ss	Kaeding
lf	Izzerson
c	Maul
cf	Rolfus
2b	Gerrmotti
rf	Phillips
1b	Claus
p	Gaston

Central City

ss	E. Mahoney
cf	Nielson
3b	Holmes
c	Mickel
1b	Davis
2b, rf	J. Mahoney
p	Buck
rf	Ritchie
lf	Campbell